SCHOLASTIC

D0784483

The Primary Teacher's Guide to

Grammar and Punctuation

• Key subject knowledge • Background information • Teaching tips •

Sebastien Melia

Book End, Range Road, Witney, Oxfordshire, OX29 0YD

www.scholastic.co.uk

© 2012 Scholastic Ltd

23456789 345678901

British Library Cataloguing-in-Publication Data
A catalogue record for this book is available from the British Library.

ISBN 978-1407-12784-2
Printed and bound by CPI Group (UK) Ltd, Croydon, CR0 4YY

Due to the nature of the web, we cannot guarantee the content or links of any site mentioned. We strongly recommend that teachers check websites before using them in the classroom.

Author
Sebastien Mella

Commissioning Editor
Rachel Mackinnon

Development Editor
Melissa Rugless

Assistant Editor
Sarah Sodhi

Icons
Tomek.gr

Series Designers
Shelley Best and Sarah Garbett

Every effort has been made to trace copyright holders for the works reproduced in this book, and the publishers apologise for any inadvertent omissions.

MIX
Paper from
responsible sources
FSC® C013604

Contents

Information within this book is highlighted in the margins by a series of different icons. They are:

Subject facts
Key subject knowledge is clearly presented and explained in this section.

Why you need to know these facts
Provides justification for understanding the facts that have been explained in the previous section.

Common misconceptions
Identifies and corrects some of the common misconceptions and beliefs that may be held about the subject area.

Vocabulary
A list of key words, terms and language relevant to the preceding section. Vocabulary entries appear in the glossary.

Amazing facts
Interesting snippets of background knowledge to share.

Teaching ideas
Outlines practical teaching suggestions using the knowledge explained in the preceding section.

Handy tips
Specific tips or guidance on best practice in the classroom.

Grammar and Punctuation

The purpose of this book is to provide teachers with basic information about grammar and punctuation. It has been written in response to the anxieties felt by many teachers who were not taught these aspects of language during their own schooldays, and who now find themselves in the position of having to teach the subjects themselves. Set out below is a rationale for each of the areas covered.

Grammar

The traditional teaching of grammar is a controversial area and fell from favour altogether in the 1960s when it was seen as suffocating rather than fostering an interest in the workings of language. Unfortunately, the discredited practices were not replaced by alternative approaches to language study.

However, there has since been much classroom-based research suggesting that investigative approaches to grammar and punctuation can help develop knowledge of concepts and terminology. These approaches focus learners' attention on how speech and writing are used in social contexts. For example, children are encouraged to think about the ways in which people talk to each other in various settings; or the ways in which writing is used in fiction, non-fiction, advertising and other forms of environmental print.

This research has helped to clarify the rationale for teaching children about grammar and punctuation:

● Language is an essential aspect of human life and, therefore, deserves to be studied in its own right, whether or not such study has a pragmatic spin-off in improving aspects of language performance.

● Exploring everyday talk and writing can inspire children's curiosity about language, persuading them to take a more attentive and critical attitude towards their reading, writing, listening and viewing. In order to support such an approach, teachers need a basic understanding of how language is structured.

● As accomplished adults, teachers use structures and conventions in their writing and speech without realising how complex and potentially confusing these can be for learners (particularly those learning English as an additional language). One of the recurrent aims of this book is to alert teachers to the fact that children's errors often signal attempts to use new and challenging constructions, and may, therefore, be seen as signs of growth rather than weakness or carelessness.

The account of grammatical analysis set out in this book is based on the model outlined by Katharine Perera in her classic work, *Children's Writing and Reading: Analysing Classroom Language* (Basil Blackwell/André Deutsch Ltd), published in 1984. The teaching suggestions, which follow the informational sections within each chapter, seek as far as possible to encourage an investigative and playful approach to language study.

Punctuation

This topic has not been as controversial as that of grammar, largely because it has been ignored and treated as nothing more than an irritant for both teachers and learners. Because very little longitudinal research has been done into the learning of punctuation, the objectives for punctuation use, introduced by the National Curriculum in 1990, were based on guesswork about what it is reasonable for children to be able to do at various stages in their school years.

This 'common sense' approach to punctuation pays little heed to the complexities of the subject. Although punctuation marks are highly familiar conventions, it is notoriously difficult to define exactly how they should be used. The traditional notion that they mark different pause lengths in the recitation of a written text excludes many of the marks and fails to take account of the fact that they structure chunks of meaning rather than just stretches of potential speech. Though the declamatory function of punctuation is rooted in the history of oratory, most texts nowadays are written for silent reading. The picture is also complicated by the fact that punctuation conventions are far more flexible than, for example, spelling conventions. Usage has changed quite drastically from generation to generation. Within certain limits, the same text can be punctuated differently by different writers and still convey the same meaning effectively. In other words, punctuation is governed by choice within flexible rules.

The sections within the punctuation chapter set out these flexible rules indicating, where appropriate, options for alternatives. The role of punctuation in clarifying the meaning of the words set down by the writer is explored in the activities in the suggestions for teaching, where children are encouraged to examine how the different marks are used in the texts that surround them, and how meaning can be modified by playing with alternative patterns.

Because punctuation is crucial in indicating the grammatical relationships within sentences, there is a lot of useful overlap between the material in this chapter and that in earlier chapters.

Sentences, clauses and phrases

There is a sense in which sentences are the most basic grammatical unit. The task that grammarians set themselves is to explain the rules by which smaller units, such as words and phrases, cohere into intelligible sentences. Accordingly, this chapter presents an overview of the rest of the book. Key concepts such as clause elements, word classes, coordination and subordination are mentioned here and are then returned to in the remaining chapters. It is essential, therefore, that the ideas in this chapter are understood before you move on to the rest of the book, as they will be revisited many times.

Sentences

Subject facts

Trying to define a sentence is a bit like trying to define a game. There are several criteria which make an activity qualify as a game, but no criteria apply to all games. Try explaining how we can say that an elderly lady setting out cards in a game of patience is doing the same kind of thing as a group of young men weltering in mud on a rugby pitch. Then try explaining why a one-word command such as *Eat!* is the same kind of thing as a complex statement such as *Leeks, garlic, shallots and chives, although dissimilar in size, shape and colour, all belong to the Alliaceae family.*

Perhaps the most important thing about a sentence is that it makes recognisable sense to another user of the language in which it is written. *Jack and Jill went up the hill* is a sentence, as is

There ain't no gold in them there hills. However, *Jack up Jill hill and the went* is not a sentence, and neither is *There no gold them in hills there ain't.*

In spite of a long history of attempts by linguists and teachers to define sentences, there are surprisingly few other facts about sentences which are undisputed. Most traditional definitions of sentences mention the following features:

- A sentence always contains a main verb.
- A sentence begins with a capital letter and ends with a full stop.
- A sentence 'sounds finished' or expresses a complete thought.

There are problems with all three of these criteria. Although in most sentences all words relate in some way to a root verb, there are many grammatical sentences (*Down with school! How about a bag of fish and chips?*) which contain no verbs. Some of the word strings that we find between capital letters and full stops (or question and exclamation marks) are fragmentary, or rely for their sense on previous parts of the text, as in the 'reply' section in the example below:

What do we need to make porridge? Oats, salt and water.

The 'complete thought' criterion is rather vague and intuitive; a set of words which constitute a complete thought for one person (*Manchester United, For sale, Pie and mash*) might not be accepted as a sentence by traditionalists.

Furthermore, many authors deliberately depart from traditional patterns in order to make a rhetorical point:

Jason sat down and for the first time in his life ate all of his carrots. Every last one of them.

The verbless structure of the second 'sentence' is unorthodox, but defensible because it reinforces the sense of the first.

In spite of these exceptions and confusions, the three criteria mentioned above are widely enough applicable to give you a reasonably good framework for deciding if sentences are well formed. But you also need to know that a pattern of words which fails to meet one or more of them is not necessarily ungrammatical. You need to consider why the structure in question does not meet one or other of the criteria. Sometimes it will be for deliberate effect, as in the unpunctuated poetry of ee cummings, and sometimes it will be because an error has been made.

Why you need to know these facts

● It is important for children to learn to organise their writing into sentences and so it is important for teachers to be able to see sentence structures emerging and to know when children need guidance in refining these structures.

Vocabulary

Phrase – a string of words acting as a clause element. A phrase is named after the word class of its main word or head.
Sentence – a string of words consisting of at least one clause, expressing a statement, question, imperative or exclamation.
Verb – a clause element identifying an action, state or relationship.

Amazing facts

A sentence can be of any length. A single word can constitute a sentence (see above). At the other extreme, it's theoretically possible to extend a sentence to infinity, with the full stop indefinitely deferred. Consider the recursive structure within a traditional rhyme such as 'The House That Jack Built':

This is the house that Jack built.
This is the malt that lay in the house that Jack built.
This is the rat that ate the malt that lay in the house that Jack built.

The traditional version extends the sentence to 13 clauses, but there is no reason why we should not continue to extend it 'ad infinitum'. The same principle can be applied to any sentence but, in practice, sentence length is constrained by common sense, with the writer being aware that the longer a sentence is, the harder it is to understand.

Common misconceptions

You may have been taught at school that it's wrong to begin a sentence with the words *and, but* and *because,* or to end a sentence with a preposition. Many teachers are surprised to discover that these prescriptive rules are relatively recent inventions, and have no validity. A fairly casual browse through published speeches and other forms of literature will show that both 'rules' are regularly broken by the most respectable writers. The first of these rules is an oversimplification. Consider the following sets of examples.

Set A
I like baked beans. But only on toast.

I went on the swings. And then on the slide.

I thought it was my brother. Because he had a blue shirt on.

Set B
Many people think that in good English writing, no sentence should begin with a conjunction. But this is not the case.

Andy was a learned scholar, a gifted poet, a considerate gentleman and a courageous warrior. And he could cook.

Indian elephants are immensely strong, intelligent and gentle. Because of this, they have been domesticated and used as beasts of burden.

In Set A, the full stop is probably inappropriate. The writer has most likely started with a 'complete thought', then added an afterthought after prematurely closing the original sentence. In Set B, the conjunction at the beginning of each sentence is used very consciously to highlight the relationship (contrast, addition, consequence) between the two sentences.

The 'rule' about not ending sentences with prepositions was invented in the 18th century by grammarians who believed that English would be a better language if it behaved more like Latin. Attempts to obey this rule often produce contorted language. (Compare *What are you looking at?* with *At what are you looking?* Then try to recast the preposition in a sentence such as *The bed hadn't been slept in.*)

Teaching ideas

● Ask the children to collect opening sentences from a range of books and to consider how the writers use them to capture readers' the attention.

● Make a recording of somebody speaking informally. Two or three minutes will be sufficient. Transcribe the recording (it will take longer than you think) and show it to the children. Discuss the ways in which the patterns of speech differ from those of writing.

● Take various sentences and scramble the word order. Ask the children to reconstruct them. This is best done with sentences which relate to current interest. It also helps if the words can be reordered in more than one way. Explore how altering the order alters the meaning.

● Collect newspaper and magazine headlines and compare them with full sentences from the text of the article. How do the headlines differ? Are they misleading or is the text that is expected 'delivered'?

● Make a collection of proverbs, headlines, political and advertising slogans, catchphrases, 'one-liners', epitaphs, public notices, famous last words, first and last lines from poems and novels – the entire print and oral environment is your best resource for exploring sentences. Encourage the children to contribute to the collection. This should help to demonstrate

the characteristic role of the sentence in encapsulating a limited, self-contained expression or piece of information.

● Collect as many children's books from as wide a range of historical periods as you can. The changes in the structure and content of sentences should be quite striking and can be used to inspire ideas for further investigations.

● Work with a matrix like the one below and encourage the children to add to it.

The	vixen	ate	the	rooster.
My	mother	painted	our	portraits.
Some	children	wrote	their	names.
His	dog	terrified	her	kitten.

What types of word can go into each column? What kinds of problems are encountered in combining words from different rows? What new columns might be added?

Types of sentence

Subject facts

Traditionally, sentences have been divided into four types:
- statements
- questions
- commands (also known as imperatives or directives)
- exclamations.

Statements

Statements assert facts or opinions, and are the most common type of sentence. They usually have a subject, the entity that the sentence is about, followed by a predicate, which provides information about the subject. The predicate consists of a verb alone or a verb followed by further sentence components:

Subject	Predicate
Garlic	stinks.
Garlic	smells lovely.
Garlic, leeks and shallots	are members of the onion family.
Some nutritionists	claim that garlic is good for you.

Questions

Questions are sentences that usually demand some kind of reply. In spoken English they are marked by rising intonation when they are genuine (*Was it you who was playing the fool last night?*) but not when they are rhetorical (*Isn't life a funny business?*). In writing they are marked by a question mark.

There are three main types of question:

- Yes/no questions can be answered with yes or no. They usually begin with an auxiliary verb such as *is, have* or *do,* or a modal verb such as *could, would* or *will.*
- 'Wh-' questions begin with an interrogative word: *who(ever), whom, whose, what(ever), which, when(ever), where(ver), why(ever)* or *how.* These questions demand a more extended response.
- Alternative questions contain a choice of answers. *Do you prefer beer, wine or water? Shall we drive there or walk?* It is of course possible to give an answer which rejects the alternatives provided by the question: *I'm not thirsty. I think we should get the bus.*

In the written form, all three types usually involve inversion of the subject and a main or auxiliary verb. *We are going shopping* = *Are we going shopping?* Some sentences require use of the auxiliary verb *do. He likes to go shopping* = *Does he like to go shopping?* In speech, inversion is optional and questions can be formed simply by a rising intonation: *We're going shopping?*

Commands

Commands usually omit the subject of the sentence (the person to whom the command is addressed, normally the second person pronoun *you*), and can be expressed as 'bare' verbs, or verbs followed by objects and/or adverbials (these terms will be explained later, but you can get a feel for their meaning by looking at the examples):

Run!	V
Finish quickly.	V + Adv
Do your homework as quickly as you can.	V + O + Adv clause
Toss the cat another goldfish.	V + Ind O + DO

V = verb
Adv = adverb
O = object
Ind O = indirect object
DO = direct object

Exclamations

These are sentences that express surprise or strong emotion, and are denoted in writing by the use of the exclamation mark. The word order of an exclamation may be the same as that of a corresponding statement, question or command, so the punctuation mark is crucial in giving the sentence its intended force. Compare the potential meanings of the following pairs of sentences:

That's the stuff.
That's the stuff!

Leave me alone.
Leave me alone!

Did you see that?
Did you see that!

Note also that many exclamations belong to the class of verbless sentences:

What a splendid tart!
How about that for a laugh!

Why you need to know these facts

● There is probably nothing in the section above that you didn't know already, but it's often beneficial to have some of the complexities of English that we normally take for granted pointed out in a systematic manner. This is particularly important if you are dealing with young children, who may be at the early stages of learning these complexities. There is also the important complicating factor that in many educational settings we use the grammatical form of a question, statement or exclamation in order to convey a command in a less forceful manner:

Would you like to give Lucy a turn on the xylophone, Ravi?
There's an awful lot of pencils on the floor.
What a loud voice!

Children who are unaccustomed to these pragmatic variations may interpret them literally, and consequently appear ruder than they intend. For example, Ravi might interpret his teacher's enquiry as a *genuine* question, rather than a concealed command, and reply with a simple 'No'.

Vocabulary

Adverb – a word which can modify a verb, an adjective or another adverb: *He walked* **quickly**; *he felt* **extremely** *uncomfortable; he breathed* **quite** *rapidly.* Adverbs can also join sentences together or provide a comment on the content of a sentence: **Consequently**, *he became tired quickly.* **Frankly**, *I became impatient.*
Adverbial – a clause element consisting of a word, phrase or clause which provides information about the verb in a sentence. Adverbials are usually optional in sentences, but some verbs

would be incomplete without them: *Dinner lasted* **until midnight**. *She put the crumble* **in the oven**.

Auxiliary (helping verb) – verbs which occur with main verbs, serving to indicate aspect or modality.

Conjunction – a word which joins together words, phrases or clauses within sentences.

Imperative – a sentence form expressing an order or directive. The subject is usually deleted.

Object – a clause element usually following the subject and verb and identifying either the entity which has been affected by the verb (the direct object) or the recipient of the action (the indirect object): *I gave* **the soup** *(DO)* *to* **Charlie** *(IO)*.

Predicate – the string of words following the subject of a sentence, consisting of at least a verb and frequently an object, complement and adverbial.

Preposition – a word occurring before a noun or noun phrase showing how the noun is related to other elements in the sentence.

Pronoun – a word that is used to replace a preceding noun or noun phrase.

Subject – a clause element usually preceding the predicate and identifying the theme, topic or agent of the sentence. In passive sentences the subject is the entity affected by the verb.

Teaching ideas

● As a prelude to any new area of study, encourage the children to write as many statements as they can reflecting what they already know about the subject area. They can then write as many questions as they can, identifying what they want to find out. Putting statements and questions alongside each other can highlight the differences in form.

● Ask the children to pretend that the wisest person in the world is coming to school tomorrow. Can they write ten questions that they would most like to have the answers to?

- Try to write five statements that sum up the most important things about yourself. Challenge the children to do the same.

- At the beginning of the school year, decide on some agreed rules of behaviour with the children and display them as a set of 'class commandments'.

- Explore more examples of statements, questions and exclamations being used as disguised commands. Discuss ways in which these might lead to misinterpretation. Remember that adults sometimes use such devices among themselves. The sentence *Are you going out dressed like that?* for example, looks like a question, but implies a statement (*You look ridiculous*), could act as a command and, if spoken more forcefully, could be an exclamation!

- Discuss ways in which the intonation of spoken sentences can distinguish between statements, questions, commands and exclamations. For example, pronounce the sentence *You are going to pass your driving test* in four different ways, one for each type of sentence.

- Collect examples of the way in which people being interviewed, particularly politicians, seek to avoid straight answers to yes/no questions. This can lead to valuable classroom discussion on manipulative uses of language.

- Encourage the children to look for examples of rhetorical questions in advertising and the media, and for 'commands' in public notices, road signs and sets of instructions. Tabloid headlines are often in the form of exclamations, especially on the sports pages. These examples of environmental print could contribute to a resource bank or display.

Clauses and clause structure

Subject facts

Although sentences can take the form of statements, questions, commands and exclamations, statements are considered to be the basic type from which the other sentence types are derived by the processes outlined above (for example, inverting the subject and verb to make a question, and deleting the subject to make a command). In examining the structure of sentences, statements are the most convenient starting point, and will be used in all the examples below.

What is a clause?

The first point to notice is that sentences consist of one or more clauses. These are self-contained units, usually consisting of a subject and predicate. You should be able to identify three clauses in the sentence below:

The table was spread, the food was ready, and the band began to play.

Each of these separate, potentially independent groups of words is a clause. The division of clauses into subject and predicate has already been demonstrated. We have seen that a predicate consists of at least a verb (*Garlic* **stinks**); the verb can, however, be accompanied by other elements: objects, adverbials and complements. These are all clause elements.

Basic finite clause patterns

The different ways in which these clause elements combine give us seven basic patterns.

Subject + verb (SV)

subject	verb
The band	played.
The hungry audience	listened.
My appreciative friends	applauded.

Subject + verb + object (SVO)

subject	verb	object
Several noisy diners	were rattling	their cutlery.
Six of the percussionists	performed	a drum roll.
My children	were devouring	all the bread rolls.

The object usually denotes the entity 'affected' by the verb.

Subject + verb + complement (SVC)

subject	verb	complement
Our first course	was	deep-fried cod.
The bandleader	was looking	ravenous.
The customers	remained	impatient.

Note that the subject and the complement refer to the same entity: the *first course* and the *cod* are the same thing; the qualities of ravenousness and impatience are used to tell us more about the bandleaders and the customers (a useful mnemonic is to think of the complement 'completing' the subject). Therefore, the most typical verb in an SVC clause is the verb *be* or alternatives such as the ones above, which perform a similar function. Other possibilities include *seem, appear, become, smell* and *taste*.

Subject + verb + object + indirect object (SVOO)

subject	verb	direct object	indirect object
Alice	threw	an olive and an anchovy	to the violinist.
He	played	a passionate cadenza	for her.
The manager	offered	a job	to my friend.

The indirect object is often described as the 'recipient' of the direct object. The order of the two objects is usually interchangeable; if the indirect object follows the verb, the preposition in front of it is usually omitted:

Alice threw the violinist an olive and an anchovy.
He played her a passionate cadenza.
The manager offered my friend a job.

Subject + verb + object + complement (SVOC)

subject	verb	object	complement
I	found	the chutney	particularly tempting.
My partner	declared	her risotto	fragrant but inedible.
The manager	made	my friend	head waiter.

In this type of clause, the complement identifies with (or completes) the object rather than the subject. As with SVC clauses, only a small number of verbs can occupy the V slot. Other possibilities include *name, consider* and *deem*.

Subject + verb + adverbial (SVA)

subject	verb	adverbial
The xylophonist	improvised	very beautifully.
A flower-seller	strode	towards our table.
We	left	when the last song was over.

The adverbial acts like a complement to the verb. Its main role is to provide information about the when, where and how of the verb. Although the role of the adverbial clause element is often performed by an adverb or an adverb phrase (as in the first example), other constructions, such as prepositional phrases (second example) and subordinate clauses (third example), can also do this job. These constructions will be examined in more detail in later chapters.

Subject + verb + object + adverbial (SVOA)

subject	verb	object	adverbial
The vigorous young trumpeters	put	their mouthpieces	to their lips.
A team of waiters	placed	the loaded trays	on the groaning table.
The boy scout	rested	his head	against the wall.

It is interesting to note that in these examples, the sentences would sound incomplete without the adverbial (check this by covering up the last column). Only a handful of verbs in English require both objects and adverbials. Adverbials are more often optional elements, which enjoy a great degree of mobility within the clause:

*The hog turned on the spit **slowly and voluptuously**.*
*The hog, **slowly and voluptuously**, turned on the spit.*
***Slowly and voluptuously**, the hog turned on the spit.*

Other clause elements are relatively fixed in relation to each other, though we can swap them about to a limited extent for emphasis:

I love venison sausages. (SVO)
Venison sausages I love. (OSV)

Non-finite and verbless clauses

In the examples so far, the verb has been finite – that is, its form has been dependent on the time of the action (tense) and the number of the subject. For example:

Time
I *run* an efficient kitchen. (present)
I *ran* an efficient kitchen. (past)

Number
I *work* in the fast-food restaurant. (first person)
She *works* in the fast-food restaurant. (third person)

This will be covered in more detail in Chapter 2, but in the meantime, look at how the verb changes in these examples:

> I *freeze* lamb burgers.
> He *freezes* lamb burgers.
> Michelle *froze* the lamb burgers.

However, there are forms of the verb that do not change according to tense and number. In the example below, the forms *freezing, to freeze* and *frozen* can be used regardless of the tense and number expressed in the rest of the sentence:

I/(s)he	am/is/was/will be	freezing the lamb burgers.
I/(s)he	want(s)/wanted/will want	to freeze the lamb burgers.
Once frozen,	a/the lamb burger(s)	lose(s)/lost/will lose flavour.

A clause centred on a non-finite verb form is known as a non-finite clause. Non-finite clauses are used as subordinate clauses (see Chapter 3) and they frequently omit the subject:

Being a vegetarian ecologist, I find the very idea of a lamb
burger repulsive.
The burgers smell delicious **when cooked**.
Every summer, **to taste good lamb**, we go to Somerset.

Another type of clause which can act as a subordinate clause is
the verbless clause. This might be a puzzling term, since we have
said that clauses should contain a subject and a predicate, and a
predicate must contain at least a verb. In the verbless clause, the
verb has been deleted for reasons of economy, but we can still
'feel' its unstated presence:

Their brush with extinction over, the buffaloes roam the great
plains once more.
The lamb masala, **when available**, is majestic.
Dick's got more salad in his burger **than Harry**.

Why you need to know these facts

● Knowledge of the different roles played by words and phrases
and how these can be structured into sentences can help to give
you insights into text complexity. This applies to both the texts
that children read, and those that they produce themselves.

● The number of different clause structures in a child's speech
or writing is one measure of the child's grammatical development
(see also the section on coordination and subordination on
pages 103–111).

● Note that there is no need for children at primary level to be
taught the technical details of clause structure given above, and
the abstractions involved are likely to be confusing. However, it
is useful to provide children with opportunities for playing with
structures within sentences, shifting their positions, altering the
content and noting the effects on meaning.

Sentences, clauses and phrases

Vocabulary

Adverb phrase – a phrase in which the main word or head is an adverb.

Clause – a potentially independent string of words consisting of at least a subject and a predicate.

Complement – a clause element which completes the meaning of either the subject or object in a sentence: *Elsie is **a baker**; she considers her loaves **exceptionally nutritious**.* The first bold element is a subject complement; the second an object complement.

Finite/non-finite – a finite verb form changes according to tense: *He eats regularly; he ate a good meal every hour on the hour.* A non-finite form does not express tense: *Having eaten, he drank; having eaten, we will relax.*

Prepositional phrase – a phrase consisting of a preposition followed by a noun phrase.

Subordinate clause – a clause in a complex sentence which is dependent on a main clause. (See complex sentence.)

Tense – variation in verb form to express the time frame of an action or event.

Teaching ideas

● Play substitution and expansion games with each of the seven clause types, starting with clauses in which each element is represented by a single word. Use a substitution matrix like the one suggested in the section on sentences (see page 14).

● Prepare texts in which the sentences consist of just one or two types of clause and compare them with texts in which the mix is richer. Help the children to identify the effects of each type of text. Discuss why these effects occur and help the children to apply the ideas explored to their own writing.

● Old reading schemes often have stories in which the grammatical complexity as well as the vocabulary have been strictly controlled. It might be interesting to look at these with older children and to see if they can assess how the distinctive flavour of these texts is produced.

Phrases

Subject facts

The word 'phrase' is one of the most difficult grammatical terms to define precisely. This is because grammarians use it in different ways. Its most common everyday usage, as in *a phrase book of Spanish* suggests that a phrase can be any item of language, from a single word to a whole sentence. In traditional school grammar, a phrase is defined as a group of words that 'hold a specific office' in a sentence, but do not contain a finite verb. However, in formal grammatical description, the word 'phrase' is applied to any word or groups of words (including traditionally defined phrases) which do a particular job in a sentence, including those which do the job of the verb. Some grammarians even suggest that as a whole sentence does a particular job, and could theoretically be used as a component in a longer sentence, the sentence itself should also be regarded as a phrase. Let's look at these two uses of the word separately.

Traditionally defined phrases

Older grammar books define a phrase as a group of words which do a particular job in a sentence, but do not make sense on their own and do not contain a finite verb:

*Last night I heard **a beautiful nightingale** singing.*
*The river flowed **through a deep valley**.*
*The slogan **on his T-shirt** made no sense.*
***Bit by bit**, the sea chewed the cliff away.*

In this classification, phrases are contrasted with clauses, which also do specific jobs in sentences, but do contain finite verbs, and may make sense on their own (see the section on clauses on pages 20–26).

Contemporary grammatical description

In more modern grammars, a phrase is a single word or, more typically, a group of words which do a particular job in a sentence, including the job of the verb. In other words, they are 'realisations' of the clause elements that have been outlined above. If you look down the columns for each of the clause elements in the tables on pages 20–23 – subject, verb, object, complement and adverbial – you will see that these roles are sometimes realised by a single word, and sometimes by a group of words.

The main types of phrase are outlined below; they will be looked at in more detail in the next chapter.

● **Noun phrases:** These consist of a noun, a pronoun or a group of words in which the noun is the most important element:

> **Fish** *are nutritious.*
> **They** *can be deep-fried, steamed or eaten raw.*
> *Why not try* **a delicious plate of mackerel fried in oatmeal?**

Noun phrases can act as subjects, objects, subject complements and object complements.

● **Verb phrases:** The main word in a verb phrase is a verb:

> *Kippers and bloaters* **are** *smoked fish.*
> *They* **have been eaten** *in this country for centuries.*
> *They* **might have been introduced** *to Britain by the Vikings.*

● **Adverb phrases:** The main word in an adverb phrase is an adverb:

> *I eat fish* **often.**
> *I cook them* **very carefully indeed.**
> *I could eat some fish* **right now.**

Confusingly perhaps, the adverb phrase is not the only way of realising the adverbial clause element. When the adverbial is providing information about the time of the verb, it is common for a noun to be the main word:

> *The fisherman worked* **all night.**

● **Prepositional phrases:** These consist of a preposition followed by a noun phrase and can play the part of adverbial phrases. Prepositional phrases can also be used to expand noun phrases. In the first example below, the prepositional phrase expands the noun phrase; in the others, it is acting as an adverbial:

> The fish **in the oven** is sizzling beautifully.
> I can't wait to get it **on my plate**.
> It should be ready to eat **between six and six fifteen**.

● **Adjective phrases:** The most important word in an adjective phrase is an adjective. It might be preceded by a modifying adverb, such as *very, scarcely* or *extremely*, and it might be followed by a prepositional phrase:

> Salma looks **tired**.
> She seems **barely awake**.
> Usually she's **good at conversation**.

The adjective phrase, as in the examples above, is another way to realise the complement clause element.

Coordination of phrases

Each of these phrase types can be coordinated to produce a longer phrase of the same type:

> **Six glistening oysters and a shovelful of mussels** clustered on my plate.
> The hog **sizzled and sweltered and dripped** on its spit.
> Crabs should be boiled **swiftly but thoroughly**.
> He was crawling **round the kitchen on his hands and knees**.
> Good cod is **as rare as rocking horse manure and much more tasty**.

Why you need to know these facts

● One reason for being aware of the rather complicated and confusing usages of the simple word '*phrase*' is to rid yourself of the notion that there is one unified system of grammar which neatly describes the whole of the English language. Different authorities have offered different descriptions of how language works, and it is important to realise that this process is continuing.

Vocabulary

Adjective – a word expressing an attribute of a noun, for example *a ripe banana.* Adjectives are usually gradable: *ripe, riper, ripest.* These grades are respectively known as the absolute, comparative and superlative forms of the adjective.

Adjective phrase – a phrase in which the main word or head is an adjective.

Noun – a word which usually names people, places, things and ideas.

Noun phrase – a phrase in which the main word or head is a noun.

Verb phrase – a phrase in which the main word or head is a verb.

Teaching ideas

● Collect as many examples as you can of the different types of phrases listed above. Start off with a single-word example, and try to get the children to expand it as far as they can. You will find that noun phrases are almost infinitely expandable, the others much less so. Which is the most limited in its scope for expansion?

● Take a simple sentence such as *The cat sat on the mat* and encourage the children to see how it can be expanded by taking one word at a time and substituting phrases for it:

The black cat sat on the mat.
My old grey flea-bitten cat sat on the mat.
The fat tabby who strayed in from No-man's-land sat on the mat.

The cat was sitting on the mat.

The cat had been sitting on the mat.
The cat will have been sitting on the mat.

The cat sat on the tattered mat.
The cat sat on the richly embroidered Persian carpet.
The cat sat on the rug that my dad threw out in a temper.

(Note that the third examples in sets one and three above show
how a noun phrase can include a clause containing a finite verb.
This again highlights the different usages of the term 'phrase' in
traditional and contemporary grammar.)

● Take a complicated sentence, help the children to identify
the phrase elements and then see how the sentence can be
shortened by reducing the phrases:

*The venerable-looking Manx cat with the artificial tail was regally
ensconced on the best piece of Axminster carpet I'd ever seen in
my life.*
The cat sat on the mat.
It sat on it.

Resources

Children's Writing and Reading: Analysing Classroom Language by
Katharine Perera (Basil Blackwell/André Deutsch Ltd) is a classic
work on the development of grammar in children's speech and
writing. Its descriptive framework for grammatical analysis is clear
and comprehensive, and it provides a wealth of examples from
children's language to show how grammar develops.

Rediscover Grammar by David Crystal (Longman) is a more
technical guide to grammar.

Language Myths, edited by Laurie Bauer and Peter Trudgill
(Penguin) is a fascinating collection of papers discussing and
criticising dubious commandments about language use.

The Cambridge Encyclopedia of the English Language by David
Crystal (Cambridge University Press).

Word classes and phrase types

This chapter looks at the area of grammar traditionally known as 'parts of speech' and now more widely referred to as 'word classification'. It also examines how word classes operate in phrases, linking this topic back to the previous chapter. The first part of the chapter provides an overview of the topic as a whole, explaining some of the issues associated with traditional classification. In the following sections, each of the major word classes is briefly described. Because several of these word classes operate as the heads of phrases, the characteristics of these phrases and how they operate in clauses are also covered in this chapter. Noun phrases are given their own section.

Word classes

Subject facts

Traditional grammarians claim that there are eight 'parts of speech', usually listed as noun, verb, adjective, adverb, preposition, conjunction, article and interjection. Sometimes the article is omitted and the pronoun proposed as a separate part of speech; sometimes articles are grouped together with words such as *that*, *my* and *some* as determiners. In earlier grammars, the interjection was downgraded, and the participle named as a category separate from the verb.

The reason why most grammarians preferred to stick to eight categories gives a clue as to why this classification system is so fuzzy and changeable. About two thousand years ago, Dionysius Thrax, a grammarian working in Alexandria, analysed ancient

Greek into eight parts of speech, and the categorisation became fixed in the heads of most of the grammarians who followed him. The early grammarians of English were anxious to apply classical systems to our language, whether they fitted it or not, because the classical languages were seen as high-status models to which English should conform.

The implication is that we cannot claim that there are eight parts of speech in English with the same degree of certainty that we can say that there are 60 seconds in a minute, or five fingers on the primate hand. Language is open to different types of classification. Contemporary linguists have largely abandoned the term 'part of speech', and use instead the term 'word class', categorising words by how they are placed in sentences and what endings they may acquire, rather than on commonsense functional notions based on the 'jobs' that word types do. (Others have argued that, at least for some words, we should abandon categorisation altogether, treating such words as unique items with their own patterns of distribution.) To illustrate the difference, look at the sentence below:

She poached the small, white Dover sole in a large, black iron pan.

The words *Dover* and *iron* 'feel' like adjectives, because they seem to do the same kind of job that the adjectives *white* and *black* do in telling us more about the fish and the pan in which the unfortunate creature was cooked. From a formal point of view, however, this can be disputed on the grounds that neither *Dover* nor *iron* can acquire the endings '-er' and '-est', or the preceding words *more* and *most*, to show degrees of intensity; neither can they be intensified by adverbs such as *very* or *extremely*. We can say:

That was the smallest meal on the biggest plate I've ever seen.

But we cannot say:

That sole was Doverer than the one I had last week, so I cooked it in my ironest pot.

Accordingly, the words *Dover* and *iron* might be better classified as quasi-adjectival nouns, modifying the main nouns that they precede.

Why you need to know these facts

● This distinction between formal and notional classifications of word types is not one which we have to worry about too much in the primary school. What matters is not so much getting children to assign words to particular classes (as in 'Underline all the adjectives in this passage'), as getting them to recognise that certain words behave in similar ways and to use this knowledge in their reading and writing.

● In helping children to analyse and develop speech and writing, teachers need to share with them a commonly understood technical vocabulary. However, it is useful to know that the traditional 'parts of speech' terminology is problematical, and that oversimplifications can be confusing.

Vocabulary

Determiner – a word occurring before a noun, indicating whether it is definite, indefinite, singular, plural and so on, for example *a, the, our, these, both, each* and *every*.

Participle – participles are words derived from verbs but serving additional functions. The '-ing' participle is often known as the present participle and can be used as an adjective and noun: *I bought her a **fishing** rod because she loves **fishing**.* The '-ed' participle is known as the past participle and can be used as an adjective: *The **baked** trout was sumptuous.*

Amazing facts

Many words can act in more than one role, depending on the sentences in which they occur. A frequently cited example is *round*, which can act as five different parts of speech:

> The smell of the fresh loaf made me turn **round**. (adverb)
> The pizza was baked on a **round** clay platter. (adjective)
> Mum gave me another **round** of toast. (noun)
> The aroma drifted **round** the corner of the street. (preposition)
> The trawler will **round** the headland any minute now. (verb)

Teaching ideas

● A traditional and fairly simple way of familiarising children with the idea that words fall into categories based on how they are used in sentences is to provide a sentence and ask children to suggest substitutions for each of its components. For beginners, it is best to start with a simple sentence:

> The old man skilfully baked a beautiful loaf.

For the first word, we can substitute *an, this, that, one, my* and so on. These words are known as determiners, and include the more traditional categories of definite and indefinite articles.

Old can be replaced by *young, stupid, handsome, green, greedy* and so on. These words are adjectives.

Man can be replaced by a vast range of words including *woman, baker, astronaut, robot* or, if we wanted to be really fanciful, words such as *mouse, ghost* or even *tree*. These words are all nouns.

Skilfully can be replaced by other adverbs, such as *carelessly, slowly, often* or *soon* and the verb that this word qualifies (*baked*) can be replaced by other verbs such as *ate, burned, bought* or *borrowed*.

An examination of the remaining words should show that they obey similar substitution patterns to the first three. In fact, once some basic categories have been identified, it can be a useful activity to play with substitutions of words within sentences. For example, if we swap nouns for nouns or adjectives for adjectives we arrive at:

The old loaf baked a beautiful man.
The beautiful man baked an old loaf.

These are bizarre sentences, but children should be able to see that in spite of their semantic oddity, they possess a syntactic integrity which disappears when we try to swap words from different word classes:

Man old the baked loaf beautiful a.

In this example, nouns and determiners have been swapped and the result is a total destruction of grammatical structure.

● Encourage the children to explore the constraints which apply to different word classes. For example, we can place several adjectives before a noun, but it would sound odd to multiply adverbs before verbs in this way, and multiplying the noun or the verb would destroy the sentence. Differences in 'membership size' can also be contemplated: there are thousands of words within the noun, verb and adjective classes, fewer in the adverb, and only a handful of determiners. Exploration of other sentences will show that the conjunction and preposition classes are also quite limited. With more confident children, you can discuss the different ways in which these 'content' words (nouns, verbs and adjectives) and 'function' words (conjunctions, prepositions and determiners) contribute to the sense of sentences.

Explorations of forms of limited or reduced language, such as baby talk, pidgins and the wording used in text messages, will show that the content words are less dispensable than the function words. If we reduce the sentence *I am hungry and want some food* to its content words, we arrive at:

hungry want food

If we reduce it to its function words we get:

I am and some

The former expression is typical of pidgin languages: those which arise from contact between groups of people who do not share a common language.

● Highlight this difference in another way by providing children with a mixture of function and content words, and asking them to define or to illustrate the words. There will not be any difficulties in doing this with most content words (also known as lexical words) but it will be very difficult with function words (also known as grammatical words).

● Encourage the children to create contexts for specified multi-purpose words, such as the following:

butter (noun, verb)
cook (noun, verb)
green (noun, adjective)
drink (noun, verb)
wet (verb, adjective)
down (noun, verb, adjective, adverb, preposition)

● Look at ways in which one part of speech can be transformed into another by the addition of affixes:

verb	affix	noun
transform		transformation
confirm		confirmation
celebrate	-ation	celebration
condense		condensation
evaporate		evaporation
noun	**affix**	**verb**
carbon		carbonise
colony		colonise
demon	-ise	demonise
terror		terrorise
crystal		crystallise
adjective	**affix**	**noun**
empty		emptiness
silly		silliness
tasty	-ness (or -iness)	tastiness
full		fullness
sweet		sweetness

● Create 'word webs' from root forms and explore how the addition of affixes can generate words from different word classes. For example, *sight: sights, sighted, sighting, sightings, insight, insightful.*

● Look at ways in which recent currents in language change have rendered the boundaries between verbs and nouns more permeable, so that words belonging to one class can be used as another, often to the displeasure of language conservatives:

*The queen went for a **walkabout** in the fast food sector.*

*The waiters here need a good **telling off**.*

*I always **bookmark** my favourite websites.*

● To reinforce the children's understanding of word functions and the way in which words go together in sentences, ask them to think of words about a specific topic, sort the words into categories and then compose sentences combining words from each category.

For example, these words were compiled by a group of children after a visit to the school pond. The teacher showed how they could be sorted into categories, and she also encouraged the composition of sentences in a shared writing session:

nouns	verbs	adjectives
water	float	sludgy
pondweed	slither	green
slugs	creep	streaky
tree stump	twitch	rotten
fungi	grow	grey

Green pondweed floats on the sludgy, grey water.

Streaky slugs slither under the rotten tree stump.

● As a variant of the previous activity, ask the children to select words from colour-coded decks of cards corresponding to different parts of speech (determiners, nouns, verbs and adjectives are useful categories to begin with). Each child in the group selects a different card, and the group as a whole has to compose a sentence, or preferably two or three sentences, in a given time.

● The exploration of jokes can be a fruitful source of discussion, as many jokes depend for their humour on the deliberate misapplication of word classes. For example:

How do you make a swiss roll?
Push him down an alp.

Here, the word *roll* has been construed as a verb rather than a noun in a compound word. Children's joke books will provide many similar examples. Make a selection and discuss them with the class.

Nouns

Subject facts

Nouns are the most numerous words in English. They serve a naming function, identifying things, concepts and persons. This function is fundamental to language, and it is significant that the first words acquired by young children seem to reflect a need to label people and events in the environment.

Most sentences contain at least one noun, often accompanied by a determiner. Within the sentence nouns can occupy a variety of slots, either on their own or as the 'head' or most important part of a noun phrase. They can be the following types:

The subject of a sentence
Potatoes are an almost miraculously nutritious food.
A large plate of sizzling roast potatoes is a delight to all the senses.

The direct object
> I like *spuds*.
> I enjoy *every variety of potato*.

The indirect object
> He gave *the potato patch* a good manuring.
> He donated much of his income to *the local chippy*.

The subject complement
> Potatoes are *tubers*.
> Potatoes can be *an excellent comfort food*.

The object complement
> Ali considered Tim *a spud-lover*.
> I nominate your mashed potato *the best in Rutland*.

Components of prepositional phrases
> He put the potato *in the microwave*.
> He placed the pan *on top of his brother's stove*.

Used in a quasi-adjectival way to modify other nouns
> I shortened my cooking time with a *microwave* oven and a *pressure* cooker.

Noun endings

In some languages, nouns are signalled by the presence of distinctive endings. For example, in Latin nouns end in '-a', '-is', or '-um' depending on their gender. In English there is no such uniformity, especially in monosyllabic nouns; however, many polysyllabic nouns – which are predominantly derived from verbs, adjectives or other nouns – are identifiable as nouns by the suffixes which have been added to them:

-ing	*I like gardening, cooking and eating.*
-er	*My father was a gardener, a miner and an amateur baker.*
-ation	*I deplore the domination of food production by multinational organisations.*
-ity	*Questions of morality are sacrificed to the demands of profitability.*
-ness	*The fattiness of a joint is in direct proportion to the richness of its flavour.*
-ism	*Environmentalism, many would claim, is a movement to control pollution.*
-ist	*He's an excellent dramatist, but a terrible rationalist.*

Other common noun suffixes are '-dom', '-hood' and '-age'.

Plurals

Most nouns can change from singular to plural, and acquire a range of suffixes in the process, but usually just an '-s' or '-es':

My husband will have a scotch egg and a baked potato; I'll have two eggs over easy and the home-fried potatoes.

Other, relatively rare ways of showing the plural in English are shown below:

Singular	Plural
loaf	loaves
ox	oxen
child	children
mouse	mice
foot	feet
woman	women
tooth	teeth
hippopotamus	hippopotami
sheep	sheep

As well as acquiring an '-s' for plural forms, nouns can also acquire an apostrophe '-**'s**' to show possession. (This is known as the genitive case of the noun.)

> This **swede's** skin is as tough as leather.

When the noun is plural, the apostrophe comes after the 's':

> The **diners'** angry voices alarmed the kitchen staff.

However, if we have a plural noun not ending in 's', the apostrophe stays before the 's':

> The **children's** appetites were gargantuan.

(See Chapter 4, pages 157–61, for detail on the apostrophe.)

Noun categories

Nouns can be divided into subcategories depending on the type of entity that they name. Proper nouns are 'given' names referring to unique entities, such as specific people, places, occasions and institutions. Common nouns are general names for whole classes of entities. Compare the following pairs of examples:

> **Jane Grigson** was an inspiring cook.
> My **cookery teacher** was also my saviour.
>
> **Southall** is a great place to buy fresh coriander.
> You are more likely to find interesting food in **towns**.
>
> On **Christmas Day** I like to feast.
> On other **public holidays** I like to fast.

In each case, the first bold example is a proper noun naming a specific entity, while the second is a non-specific common noun. Note that proper names are capitalised, and do not normally appear in dictionaries; usually, they occur without a determiner, but in figurative writing they might acquire one. Compare:

> **Shanghai** is the culinary centre of Asia, if not the world.
> Welcome to **the Shanghai** of Tyneside.

*King **Henry VIII** could eat a whole hog-roast.*
*He's a bit of a **Henry VIII** when he gets near a hog-roast.*

In this last example, the proper noun is being used as an eponym, a special type of common noun derived from a proper noun. Many of them have become so commonplace that they are no longer capitalised:

*He not only filled his belly, he filled his **wellingtons** as well.*
*There's nothing better than a dram of **grog** to wash a kipper down.*

In the first example, the bold word is derived from the proper name (Lord) Wellington, who wore distinctive boots; in the second, it is derived from Old Grogram, the nickname of the admiral who introduced the watering down of the rum ration in the Royal Navy.

Count and non-count nouns

Common nouns can be further divided into count and non-count (or mass) nouns. The former term refers to entities that can be counted as individual items: *six eggs, two apples, a thousand possibilities*. The latter term refers to entities that cannot be envisaged as countable units: *some wine, a heap of wheat, a lot of potential*. Count nouns cannot occur without a determiner in the singular, whereas non-count nouns can:

Wheat *fell from the wagon.* (non-count)

Count nouns in the singular require *a* or *an*, whereas non-counts require *some*, or another kind of quantifying word:

*I'm longing for **an apple**.* (count)

*I'd love **some cream**.* (non-count)

Count nouns can be pluralised, but non-count nouns cannot:

*There are **many possibilities** ahead for him.* (count)

The distinction between count and non-count is not always clear. Some nouns can act as either, depending on the context:

*Children eat too much **sugar**.* (non-count)
*How many **sugars** do you have in your tea?* (count)

*I prefer **water** to wine.* (non-count)
*Could I have a glass of red, a lemonade and two **waters**, please?*
(count)

There is a small but interesting set of nouns between count and
non-count nouns which identify entities, mainly lower items of
clothing which come in inseparable pairs. The most common
examples are *trousers, jeans, leggings, pants* and so on, and
from outside of the clothing range, *scissors*. These nouns, in the
singular, so to speak, can be preceded by *a pair of* or *the* but
not usually by *a* standing alone. (Though some dialects do allow
their users to say *Don't spill your soup on your pant* or *Hand me a
scissors please*.) Where paired items can be physically separated
(for example, *shoes* and *socks*) the nouns belong to the class
of counts.

Collective nouns

Collective nouns are words which refer to a number of
individuals considered as a group (*team, army, family, crowd* and
so on). As subjects in sentences, they can precede either singular
or plural forms of verb and pronoun, depending on whether one
is stressing the unity or individuality of the entities making up
the group:

*My **team** is the best in the business. It…* (singular)
*My **team** are always at each other's throats. They…* (plural)

There are also many collective nouns related to animals for
example, *gaggle* (of geese), *flock* (of sheep), *swarm* (of bees).

Concrete and abstract nouns

Common nouns can be further subdivided into concrete and
abstract. The latter refers to entities that are measurable and
at least potentially sensible, the former to general concepts
and qualities. Some relatively clear examples are given in the
following table:

concrete	abstract
onion	greed
banquet	generosity
food mixer	care
goblet	beauty
turkey	joy

As with most linguistic distinctions, there is a fuzzy boundary between these categories. The word *taste*, for example, seems abstract when we talk about the taste of food in general, or about having *a taste for apricots*; but when we mention experiencing a sweet or bitter taste, the word is used in a concrete sense. Compare the use of the noun *beauty* in the following sentences:

The beauty of the salad was matched only by its savour.

The horse was a real beauty.

Why you need to know these facts

● The technical differences between count and non-count nouns, the irregular plurals of English and other aspects of affix families may not seem to be of much relevance to primary teaching, but a knowledge of them will provide a foundation for understanding some of the complexities of English grammar, and hence some of the problems that children have in mastering it. Such knowledge is particularly vital if you are to appreciate the difficulties that many learners of English as an additional language encounter when they are trying to form plurals, or find an appropriate determiner for a noun. For all children, familiarity with the affix system will definitely help with spelling.

● The distinction between concrete and abstract nouns is an interesting one to think about when taking children through the early stages of literacy. Early oral vocabulary often consists largely of concrete nouns. There is a sound argument that one of the first tasks of the reading teacher is to establish the idea that spoken words can be represented by written words. Collections of words and pictures depicting these concrete nouns are commonly used to forge this link between spoken and written language.

● Abstract nouns include some of the most controversial words in the dictionary. If children are to become critical readers and writers, they need to be aware of this fact, and of the issues surrounding such elusive but casually wielded words as *truth, justice* and *freedom*.

● The significance of proper nouns also looms large in early literacy. Often the first words that children can read or write include their own names and addresses, and various other proper nouns, such as names of characters in favourite books or TV programmes, and the brand names of familiar products. You should take advantage of this early interest in names and naming, and also point out the difference in function and capitalisation conventions between proper and common nouns. Any activities which involve the identification, sorting and invention of proper nouns will be helpful in this respect. For example, writing and addressing letters, 'print walks' involving attention to street names and locations or inventing people and place names in story writing.

***

Amazing facts

Although English does not have a gender system for its nouns, there are still many nouns in English which denote gender, or favour one gender over another:

chairman, postman, milkman

Moves have been made over the last few decades to desexualise language in various ways, introducing such terms as:

firefighter, flight attendant, chairperson (or *chair*)

Some terms have been more successful than others. It could be interesting to discuss this issue with children and to get them to make suggestions for gender-free terminology.

Comparative linguists remind us that difference in sex is only one way in which to divide words up into genders. The word 'gender' means type, as in the biological term 'genus', and is not necessarily confined to sex; English grammars sometimes refer, for example, to differences between animate and inanimate nouns. In some languages, nouns are categorised according to: whether the items they denote occur inside or outside the home, whether they are edible or inedible, or whether they are capable or incapable of independent movement.

Teaching ideas

● Help children who are in the early stages of literacy to become familiarised with the naming function of nouns by asking them to compile personal ABCs of familiar and special objects. Daily shared reading and special events, such as 'print walks' around the school and its environs, will yield examples of proper nouns whose functions and form can be contrasted with collections of common nouns.

● Develop older children's awareness and knowledge of the spelling conventions of the affix system by asking them to make up conversion tables (see page 38) in which changes in spelling patterns can be highlighted as words switch word classes and the general rules derived through discussion.

● Allocate a variety of role-play activities to children who are learning English as an additional language and who are having difficulties with different types of plural noun or with the relationships between count and non-count nouns and their determiners. These can involve activities, either oral or written, which require the listing of objects, for example, shopping or a cupboard inventory.

● Ask the children to create pictures or stories illustrating their own interpretations of abstract nouns, such as *justice*, *friendship*, *truth* and *charity*. They can then explore texts (selected in advance) which give contrasting interpretations of these words. Collect and discuss examples of an overused word such as *quality,* which is common in advertising and political speeches. Or take newspaper articles or letters to the editor expressing opposing opinions on a topic, such as library closures or cyber-bullying, and show children how different interpretations are put on powerful abstract nouns such as *freedom* and *humanity.* Activities like these are quite challenging, but it is essential to give learners insights into the ways in which seemingly neutral words are used to serve the purposes of different groups and individuals.

Noun phrases

Subject facts

Noun phrases are the most elastic structures in the anatomy of the sentence. A noun phrase can consist of a single noun, but it can also consist of immensely long and complex strings in which function words, smaller noun phrases, prepositional phrases and even whole clauses might be chained together or embedded one within another. However, even in the longest and most complex noun phrases, one noun will be identifiable as the head of the construction. In each of the constructions below, the noun phrase is shown in bold type and the head is underlined:

The <u>diner</u> is a great place to eat.

The <u>diner</u> on Dock Road is a great place to eat.

That funny old greasy spoon <u>diner</u> on Dock Road is a great place to eat.

Many funny old greasy spoon <u>diners</u> with rickety furniture and surly staff that you can often find by chance if you are driving through the North are great places to eat.

The simplest type of multi-word noun phrase consists of a noun preceded by a definite or indefinite article, or by a similar type of determiner. The main classes of determiner are listed as follows:

the	my	your	his	her
its	our	their	no	whose
this	that	some	any	each
a	an	every	either	neither
these	those	(not) much		

As we have seen above, singular count nouns, plural count nouns and non-count nouns are preceded by different types of determiners. Furthermore, any noun can be preceded by only one of the determiners above (you can say *my apples* or *those apples*, but you cannot say *my those apples*).

Expanded noun phrases

Determiners can be preceded by quantifying words such as *half of*, *both of* and *all of*. They can be followed by ordinal words, such as *first*, *second*, *next* and *last*, and by other quantifiers, such as *many*, *most*, *few* and *several*. In between these closed class words and the head noun we can have one or more adjectives, and one or more of these adjectives can themselves be modified by an adverb, for example:

*half of the last dozen **extremely** slender green cucumbers.*

In addition to this, the noun phrase can be expanded with elements added after the head. These are commonly prepositional phrases:

*half of the last dozen extremely slender mottled green cucumbers **on the shelf**.*

They might be non-finite clauses:

*half of the last dozen extremely slender mottled cucumbers **to be harvested**.*

Or they might be finite clauses:

*half of the last dozen extremely slender mottled cucumbers, **which I grew on my allotment**.*

As post-modifying elements can themselves be modified, noun phrases can quickly grow into unwieldy verbal juggernauts:

> *half of the last dozen extremely slender mottled cucumbers,* *which I skilfully grew last year* **on my prize-winning allotment** **in Woodley**.

Two (or very occasionally more) noun phrases can be used alongside each other to express the same clause element:

> **The gherkin, a slightly comical but very lovable vegetable**, *is the cucumber's baby brother.*

In these constructions, subsequent noun phrases are said to be in apposition to the first.

It is important, though perhaps superfluous, to note that the type of expanded noun phrases we have been looking at above are far more common in writing than they are in speech. Writing offers opportunities for reflection and, therefore, for the construction of complex webs of information that are not available in spontaneous speech.

Furthermore, when people do use expanded noun phrases in their speech, they are far more likely to use them as objects, complements or in adverbial prepositional phrases than they are as subjects. Compare:

> *I like eating in* **the old greasy spoon 1980s-style diners that you can** **still sometimes find in the suburbs of London**. (SVA)

> *You can still find* **a few of those run-down rickety old transport** **cafés fringing the A40**. (SVO)

> *Jimmy's is* **one of those beautiful old places you never want to** **see close down**. (SVC)

> **The decorated tents in which you can sit down and buy a bowl** **of tea or a side of boiled sheep** *are known as guanzes.* (SVC)

While the first three extended noun phrases are roughly equivalent in complexity to the fourth one, the former sentences seem more characteristic of spoken language and the latter of written language. It has been suggested that the rarity of subject noun phrases in speech, and the difficulties that they pose to the reader, is because they contain complex information which has to be maintained in the memory before the 'point' of the sentence – expressed in the predicate – is reached. Therefore, the more information we have before the main verb, the more difficult a sentence is to process.

Why you need to know these facts

● Noun phrases are important elements in spoken and written language. One measure of oral language development is the length and complexity of the noun phrases that children produce, and their ability to use extended noun phrases in subject positions. In the field of literacy, the difficulty of the texts that children have to master is partially determined by the types and positions of the noun phrases that they encounter in them. It should be clear from the examples above that it is possible to become lost in the labyrinths of extended noun phrases, and that particular difficulties are posed when these occur in the subject position. In children's writing, progression is partially characterised by the ability to construct noun phrases.

Teaching ideas

● Collect noun phrases from various types of texts and help the children to analyse the information they convey. Try collecting noun phrases related to men and women from newspapers and compare their content.

● Noun phrases in advertising and other types of media can also be collected and compared. To guide and contextualise this type of activity, select a topic related to current school work (health, children or the environment, for example) and make an inventory of all the noun phrases related to the theme.

● Grow noun phrases by adding in all the types of constituents mentioned above. This will give children a feeling for the elasticity of the structure:

> strawberries
> fresh strawberries
> a dozen fresh strawberries
> half a dozen fresh strawberries with the dew still clinging to them

● Alternatively, present such 'exaggerated' noun phrases and reduce them down to the head noun. This is a good way of introducing the idea that all noun phrases are based on a single noun. Ask the children to discuss what the most important word is before beginning the reduction process.

Pronouns

Subject facts

'Pro-' is Latin for 'for', and the simplest way of introducing pronouns to children is to convey the idea that they often 'stand for' nouns and noun phrases (underlined):

> <u>Milk</u> is probably the most nutritious liquid in the world. **It** contains almost every ingredient essential for health.

> <u>The Earl of Sandwich</u> spent so much time gambling that **he** neglected his meals.

Pronouns can stand for one or more noun phrases (underlined):

> I chose a <u>chocolate-coated, peanut-studded, vanilla-drenched strawberry sundae</u>; **it** cheered me up enormously.

> We saw <u>orchards heavy with apples, fields of ripe corn, hedgerows full of berries</u>; **they** convinced us that the drought was over.

And they can stand for whole sentences or clauses:

> **The cherry trees had finished flowering; this** *made me realise that the fruit would soon be ready.*

There are several different types of pronoun, the most common of which is the set of personal pronouns. First-person pronouns refer to the person or persons conveying the message:

> **I** *am pleased that the committee selected* **me** *to speak.*

> **We** *were hoping that Amy could join* **us**.

Second-person pronouns refer to the person or persons being addressed:

> **You** *have only* **yourselves** *to blame.*

Third-person pronouns are used to refer to persons or other entities being written or spoken about (in this context, the impersonal 'it' is included in the class of personal pronouns):

> **He** *is a very good speaker.*

> **She** *only ever talks about* **herself**.

> **They** *are very proud of* **themselves**.

> **It** *crept under the stone.*

It also has special uses in which it does not seem to refer to anything specific at all:

> *It's raining.*

> *It seems clear that you are the culprit.*

You will note from the *I/me* and *we/us* examples above that these personal pronouns have different forms for subject and object roles. This also holds for *he* and *she*:

He asked for trouble. I gave **him** some.

She asked for water. I gave **her** nectar.

These third-person singular pronouns are gender specific; the nouns they stand for, however, need not be:

My best friend showed me how to bake bread; **she** was an expert.

The knitting champion entered the stage; **he** presented his needles to the judges.

As in the examples above, this distinction can be used for rhetorical effect in disclosing 'unexpected' gender identities.

In informal speech, personal pronouns are often used after a subject noun phrase to recapitulate or emphasise that this is to be the topic of the sentence:

<u>My mum and dad</u>, **they** took me to McDonald's.

Also in speech, a tagged-on clause centred on a pronoun is often used to recapitulate or emphasise the preceding clause:

My brother eats like a horse, **he** does.

It's the best pizzeria in Whiston, so **it** is.

Reflexive pronouns

There are nine reflexive pronouns in English: *myself, yourself, himself, herself, ourselves, yourselves, themselves, itself* and *oneself*. A sovereign using the 'royal we' may also use the term 'ourself'. Reflexive pronouns 'reflect' the action of the verb back to a noun phrase (or pronoun) in the same clause:

I gave **myself** a pat on the back.

The culprits can consider **themselves** lucky.

As in the examples above, the noun phrase is usually the subject, but reflexive pronouns can also refer to the object:

*I met **the man himself** in the Oak.*

This 'emphasising' role can also be applied to the subject:

***We ourselves** are obliged to do the deed.*

Demonstrative pronouns
The demonstrative *this, that, these* and *those* pronouns stand for objects in the speaker's environment, and imply differences in distance from the speaker:

*Give me **that** while I hand you **this**. (further/nearer)*

*I prefer **these** to **those**. (nearer/further)*

Possessive pronouns
Possessive pronouns indicate ownership:

*The paella is **mine**; the pizza is **yours**; the pasta is **theirs**; the pleasure is **ours**.*

Note that possessive and demonstrative words, often referred to as possessive and demonstrative adjectives, also occur in noun phrases:

***That** soup on the stove is **her** pride and joy.*

***Those** croutons will be **my** downfall.*

Because these words precede specified nouns, rather than standing in place of aforementioned nouns, they are acting more like determiners or adjectives than pronouns.

Interrogative pronouns
Interrogative pronouns are used to mark questions whose implied answer is a noun:

***What** are you having for breakfast today?*

***Whose** is that spectacular sandwich?*

Who has opened his lunch?

Which of the options appeals to you most?

What was that you said?

Relative pronouns

Relative pronouns are used to link subordinate clauses to the head or main word in a noun phrase (underlined):

*The American red <u>wine</u> **which** gives me most pleasure is Zinfandel.*

*The <u>rat</u> **that** ate the malt lived in the <u>house</u> **that** Jack built.*

*The <u>customer</u> **who** was complaining has left.*

Indefinite pronouns

Indefinite pronouns express unspecified quantity, extent or agency:

***Few** were worth eating.*

*I'll tell you if I see **anything**.*

***Someone** has eaten my porridge.*

Pronouns in clauses

Within clauses, pronouns, like the noun phrases they represent, can assume the role of subjects, objects and complements:

***It** was delicious. (subject)*

*I've already fed **her**. (object)*

*The honour is **mine**. (subject complement)*

*Don't call my husband **that**. (object complement)*

They can also occur in prepositional phrases acting as adverbials:

*The wine waiter stepped in **it**.*

Why you need to know these facts

● Although the pronominal system is complex, children master it fairly rapidly in their speech, and can use pronouns effectively when they are talking to familiar people in familiar circumstances. It is important not to underestimate the complexity of what has been learned. For example, young children have to learn to refer to themselves as '*I*' even though others refer to them as '*you*'; they also have to realise that in some cases they must not refer to themselves as '*I*' but as '*me*'.

● Understanding of spoken or written discourse containing pronouns requires that the listener or reader be aware of the identities of the people, places and things to which these pronouns refer. It is here that difficulties often arise when, as in educational settings, there is less shared ground between the speakers than there is at home. A sentence such as *He gave that to her and they took some of it too* is incomprehensible unless we know the references of *he, that, her, they* and *it*. Younger children, because they are relatively inexperienced communicators, often fail to indicate what such words refer to, assuming that the listener knows already. Such difficulties can be apparent up to the later stages of primary schooling.

● Lack of specificity can be even more marked in children's writing. Writing has to be more explicit than speech because the reader does not have the opportunities for clarification that occur in a conversation, nor is the reader often privy to the events being described on the page. Formal writing, in which the child is required to write in a deliberately impersonal way for an imaginary audience, is the most challenging of all. There is clearly a need for you to be aware of these difficulties, and to help children to ensure that the reference of each pronoun that they use is explicit and unambiguous.

● It is also important to be aware of what is happening when variation in pronoun usage between standard and non-standard English surfaces in children's writing. Pronouns may be used instead of determiners:

> We made one of **them** cakes they baked in the Middle Ages.

Reflexive pronouns may have variant forms:

> Jack hurt **hisself** on the swing.

> They stuffed **theirselves** with pudding.

And the subordinator *what* is frequently used as a relative pronoun:

> The recipe **what** we used came from a very old book.

Common misconceptions

Sometimes the reflexive pronoun *myself* is mistakenly used instead of the objective case personal pronoun *me*:

> The soup was prepared by Indra and myself.

By traditional standards, this usage, arising from a feeling that the use of *me* would be incorrect, is itself inappropriate.

Similarly, a reluctance to use the word *me* can lead to inappropriate uses of *I*. Traditionally, spoken forms such as *Me and my mum went to the shops* have been frowned upon because *I* is supposed to be used in the subject position. However, if the first-person pronoun is the complement of a preposition, traditional usage favours the objective form:

> **Between** you and me, I detest tofu.

> They gave the bill **to** Ella and me.

Teaching ideas

● Scan texts of various kinds, while conducting sentence-level work, to locate pronouns and to connect them back to their referents (the people or things to which they refer). This can be done by drawing arrows between the words and the noun phrases they stand for.

● Highlight the potential ambiguity of pronouns by presenting sentences to children that contain pronouns without their referents. Help the children to produce multiple interpretations of the pronouns.

● During shared or guided reading, assess examples of children's writing containing inexplicit or ambiguous referents. These can be cooperatively improved through paired writing.

● Provide the children with passages from different text genres (narratives, reports, playscripts and so on) in which pronouns have been deleted and ask the children to replace them. Discuss why some forms of pronoun are more characteristic of particular types of texts than others.

● Investigate variation in pronoun usage by collecting non-standard examples from literature, the media and the speech of the local community. Compare these with standard usage and discuss the issue of which forms are appropriate for particular contexts.

● Create a poem or dialogue consisting of language in which pronouns are used without their referents. Such texts produce a sense of mystery or puzzlement because they involve making statements about persons or things without identifying who or what these entities actually are. An excellent and very well-known example is the evidence of the White Rabbit to the trial at the end of *Alice's Adventures in Wonderland*, which begins:

> *They told me you had been to her*
> *And mentioned me to him.*

She gave me a good character,
But said I could not swim.

He sent them word I had not gone
(We know it to be true).
If she should pass the matter on,
What would become of you?

A dialogue might begin:

A: *What's that?*
B: *What's what?*
A: *That over there.*
B: *It's one of those that belong to him.*
A: *Didn't you give it to her?*
B: *No I gave one of these to her.*

Verbs and verb phrases

Subject facts

The traditional definition of a verb as a 'doing word' has long been seen as inadequate. While there are many verbs which denote action (*eat, boil, slice, pick*) there are others which express states or processes which do not have an active component (*be, seem, think, feel, forget*).

Verb phrases

Verb phrases are words or strings of words which 'realise' the verb clause element. A verb phrase can consist of a single verb or a string of words fulfilling the same function:

*My mum **is** a dinner lady.*
*My mum **has been** a dinner lady.*
*My mum **should have been** a dinner lady.*
*My mum **was going to be** a dinner lady.*
*My mum **ought to have been** a dinner lady.*
*My mum **happened to have wanted to have been** a dinner lady.*

It has often been stated that verbs are the most important words in sentences, governing relationships between all of the other words. In fact the word 'verb' is derived from the Latin *verbum*, which simply means 'word'.

Types of verbs

The most fundamental categorisation of types of verb is into main verbs (or lexical verbs) and auxiliaries (or helping verbs). Main verbs have clear independent meanings, and they can operate alone in expressing the action or state of a subject, or in connecting the subject to an object, complement or adverbial:

> *Joan* **cooks**. (SV)

> *Jean* **eats** *meat*. (SVO)

> *Jane* **seems** *hungry*. (SVC)

> *John* **dines** *frugally*. (SVA)

Lexical verbs can be subdivided according to the clause elements they accompany.

Transitive verbs

Transitive verbs (bold) require an object (underlined):

> *I* **prefer** <u>*wholemeal dumplings*</u>.

> *She* **recommended** <u>*the sea bass*</u>.

> *Alice* **devoured** <u>*the sweets*</u>.

A small number of transitive verbs (bold) require both an object and an adverbial (underlined):

> *I* **put** <u>*the dishes*</u> <u>*in the sink*</u>.

> *Lauren* **leaned** <u>*her arms*</u> <u>*against the table*</u>.

And a small number require both a direct and an indirect object (underlined):

*Lauren **gave** <u>her dessert</u> <u>to me</u>.*

Copular verbs

Copular verbs occur in sentences with complements, indicating that there is an identity with the subject. The meanings of copular verbs are usually related to the verb *be*:

*Alice **is** a good manager.*

*Lauren **seemed** inebriated.*

*The guests **became** impatient.*

Intransitive verbs

Lexical verbs which require neither objects nor complements are known as intransitive verbs. Most of them can occur with just the subject, though a small number (as in the third example) require an adverbial (underlined) as well:

*The coffee **arrived**.*

*Lauren **vanished**.*

*The waiter **stepped** <u>forward</u>.*

Many verbs can belong to more than one of these sub-classes:

*The waiter **looked** under the table.* (intransitive)
*Lauren **looked** awful.* (copular)

*The waiter **swallowed**.* (intransitive)
*Alice **swallowed** the garnish.* (transitive)

Auxiliary verbs

Auxiliary verbs cannot occur without a lexical verb, except in elliptical or abbreviated utterances. Their job is to help the main verb express such dimensions of meaning as the time reference of a sentence (tense), the completeness or duration of an action or state (aspect) and the obligatoriness, necessity or probability of a state of affairs (modality):

> Joan **must** cook.

> Jean **should** eat more meat.

> Jane **might** seem hungry.

> John **was** dining frugally.

Note that the use of an auxiliary is often accompanied by a change in the form of the main verb.

Here are some elliptical sentences in which auxiliaries occur alone:

> Jane doesn't want to cook. But she **must**.

> Jean won't eat liver. Perhaps she **should**.

> Lauren had seemed hungry. So **had** Jane.

> Who was the most frugal eater among us? John **was**.

You will see that such sentences occur most typically in speech or informal writing, and that they depend for their coherence on elements in the preceding discourse.

Auxiliary verbs are sometimes divided into primary auxiliaries (*be*, *have* and *do*) and modal auxiliaries (*can, could, may, might, must, ought, shall, should, will* and *would*). Note that *be, have* and *do* and their variant forms, such as *am, having* and *did*, are also main verbs. Compare the pairs of examples below:

> I **am** hungry. (main verb)

> I **am** _eating_ at my grandmother's house tonight. (auxiliary verb)

In the first example, a form of the verb *to be* is operating as a main verb, equivalent to a similar verb such as *feel*; in the second, it is an auxiliary to the main verb *eating*, helping to indicate tense.

> He **has** an ox tongue in his freezer. (main verb)

He **has** <u>forgotten</u> how to deal with it. (auxiliary verb)

In the first example, a form of the verb to have is operating as a main verb, equivalent to a similar verb such as possess; in the second, it is an auxiliary to the main verb forgotten, again helping to indicate tense.

Hugh **did** a jambalaya. (main verb)

I **did** <u>enjoy</u> it. (auxiliary verb)

In the first example, a form of the verb to do is operating as a main verb, equivalent to a similar verb such as prepare; in the second example, it is an auxiliary to the main verb enjoy, adding a note of emphasis.

In each of the pairs of examples, the first sentence contains only one verb, which must therefore be the main verb; the second sentence shows the same word form now acting as an auxiliary to augment the import of the main verb.

As indicated above, the modal auxiliaries express the mood of the verb, or our feeling about the possibility, obligation and tentativeness of the state of affairs it expresses. Compare the shades of meaning created by the use of modal auxiliaries in the sentences below:

I **can** prepare a meal.
I **could** prepare a meal.
I **may** prepare a meal.
I **might** prepare a meal.
I **must** prepare a meal.
I **ought** to prepare a meal.
I **shall** prepare a meal.
I **should** prepare a meal.
I **will** prepare a meal.
I **would** prepare a meal.

Modal auxiliaries are also used to mark politeness or hesitancy:

Could I offer you an aperitif?

*You **might** want to try a sharper cheese.*

Sometimes a sense of 'shouldness' or possibility is expressed by using a special form of the main verb itself, rather than a modal auxiliary. This is known as the subjunctive mood. Look at these examples and note how the form of the emboldened verb departs from its regular usage:

*If I **were** braver, I'd eat more sea urchins.*
(normal form: *If I was…*)

*Heaven **preserve** us from salmonella!*
(normal form: *Heaven preserves us…*)

*I insist he **serve** dinner instantly.*
(normal form: *…he serves…*)

*May I request that the bill **be** waived?*
(normal form: *…the bill is waived?*)

Regular verbs
Another way of classifying verbs is into regular and irregular. Regular verbs appear in four forms. The infinitive is the 'bare' or 'base' form, usually preceded by *to*, which is how the verb looks when you find it in a dictionary: *eat, cook, boil, dream, feel, think.*
    The '-s' form of the verb is used with the third person of the verb (*he, she* or *it*, or proper and common nouns corresponding to these pronouns) and usually denotes the present tense:

*Mark **feels** nauseous.*

However, it can be used to denote habitual or future action:

*The bakery **produces** bagels only on Wednesdays.* (habitual)

*He **leaves** for New York next Friday.* (future)

The '-ing' form or '-ing' participle (traditionally called the present participle) is used to convey the idea of continuous or habitual action:

*Ted is **boiling** his winkles.*

*He enjoys **toasting** marshmallows.*

Note that the term 'present' participle is potentially misleading, since this form can also be used in sentences indicating future or past time:

*I will be **boiling** my whelks as soon as I can get them ashore. (future)*

*He was **boiling** those poor clams to flavourless oblivion. (past)*

The '-ed' form or '-ed' participle (traditionally called the past participle) is used to indicate a past event, or with an auxiliary, a recently elapsed event or state of affairs:

*Rolf **devoured** the cockles.*

*Ralph has **consumed** all the winkles.*

As with the '-ing' participle, the label 'past' for the '-ed' participle can be confusing, as this form can be used in contexts indicating present or future time:

*I am **called** a glutton by all who know me. (present)*

*You will be **called** before the court next month. (future)*

Participle forms are so called because they 'participate' in the functions of other word classes. Both '-ed' and '-ing' participles can be used in an adjective-like way to modify nouns, and some '-ing' forms can also be used in a noun-like way. Compare the jobs that the participles do in the following sentences:

*Ellie has **boiled** the lobster. (verb)*
***Boiled** lobster should be served with the appropriate tool kit. (modifier)*
*Jimmy was **fishing**. (verb)*
*Jenny has a **fishing** boat. (modifier)*
*Ginger enjoys **fishing**. (noun)*

Finite and non-finite

Because they do not vary according to tense or person, the infinitive and participle forms are sometimes called 'non-finite'. This is to contrast them with 'finite' forms which vary according to particular tenses and persons. In the first two sets of sentences below, the emboldened verbs are finite: their endings depend on the preceding subject and on tense. Compare them with the uniformity of the non-finite forms (infinitive, '-ing' participle and '-ed' participle) in the last two sets:

I **like** your new kitchen.
Andrea **likes** it too.
I **liked** my greasy old den better.

You **need** a good pan to prepare an omelette.
She **needs** three large eggs for her tortilla special.
They **needed** Selma to show them how to break the eggs.

Sputtering dangerously, the bacon writhes in the pan.
Sputtering dangerously, the sausages rolled on the grill.
Sputtering dangerously, the chef burst into the dining room.

Lee enjoys **munching** brandy snaps.
Alan and Bob spend a lot of time **munching** brandy snaps.
The children were discovered **munching** brandy snaps.

Note that the word groups in which these verb forms occur are known as non-finite clauses (see Chapter 1).

Irregular verbs

Irregular verbs have '-s' and '-ing' forms similar to regular verbs, but they have irregular past-tense forms and '-ed' participles. Compare the four forms of the regular verb *swallow* with the corresponding forms of the irregular verb *eat*:

swallow	eat
Beth swallows.	Ben eats.
Beth is swallowing.	Ben is eating.
Beth swallowed.	Ben ate.
Beth has swallowed.	Ben has eaten.

There are many variants of the '-ed' form among irregular verbs. Some of them have different forms for the past tense and the past participle:

meet	met
keep	kept
take	took, taken
teach	taught
have	had
see	saw, seen
put	put
swim	swam, swum
go	went, gone
do	did, done
drink	drank, drunk

Tenses

One of the most important functions of the verb is to indicate the time of an action or state. The present tense is represented in two ways: the first uses the base form of the verb, adding '-s' for the third-person singular; the second uses one of the forms of the auxiliary *be* together with the '-ing' ending. Both ways are illustrated below:

*I **like** turkey; my sister prefers goose.*

*I **am enjoying** my guinea fowl.*

The past tense is formed with regular verbs by adding '-ed', or by using a past-tense form of *be* with the '-ing' ending:

*He **roasted** a fat duck last night.*

*He **was eating** it when I came home.*

Note also the many irregular past-tense forms in the table on page 68.

It is often stated that English does not have a future tense because the verb form does not alter when future time is indicated. Instead, auxiliaries or other word groups (bold) precede the verb (underlined):

*I **will** <u>cook</u> you the best meal you've ever eaten.*

*You **shall** <u>attend</u> the banquet.*

*You're **going** <u>to enjoy</u> this.*

*I'm **just about** <u>to eat</u>.*

As indicated above, future time can also be expressed by present-tense forms (underlined) followed by an adverbial (bold):

*The bakery <u>closes</u> **next week**.*

*The banquet <u>is happening</u> **on Friday**.*

Note also that present-tense forms can be used to indicate things that have already happened:

*Supermarket expansion **claims** another local greengrocer.*

*I hear that 'Sally's Salads' **has** gone bust.*

Aspect

Closely related to tense is the concept of aspect – the question of the completeness, duration or continuity of an action. We can distinguish two types of aspect in verb forms, the perfective and the progressive.

● **The perfective aspect:** is expressed by the verb *have* in either its present- or past-tense forms. The present perfective expresses an action or state which continues up to the present:

*We **have known** about this place since it opened.*

Compare with the past tense:

*We **knew** about the place when it opened.*

The past perfective locates the action in the past, isolating it from the present:

> I **had known** all along what was going on.

Compare with I knew or I have known.

● **The progressive aspect:** is used to indicate an action which is continuous. It uses the '-ing' form of the verb in combination with both tenses and both perfective aspects. Note the contrasts in the table below:

I cook.	present
I cooked.	past
I have cooked.	present perfective
I had cooked.	past perfective
I am cooking.	present progressive
I was cooking.	past progressive
I have been cooking.	present perfective progressive
I had been cooking.	past perfective progressive

The complexity of the tense and aspect systems is, of course, one of the major bugbears of students learning English as an additional language.

Active and passive voice

A final distinction needs to be made between the active and the passive voice. In speech, and in most written texts, it is common to use the active voice, putting the agent in the subject slot before the verb phrase, and the object or 'thing acted upon' after it:

> Chickens eat grain. (Agent VO)

> The fish swallowed the maggot. (OV Agent)

Sometimes, to create a switch of emphasis, the passive voice can be used instead. This involves moving what was the subject of the active verb to the agent slot after the verb, and adding the word *by*. The object of the active verb takes the subject slot, and the verb itself is made passive by acquiring a form of *be* and the '-ed' participle:

> *Grain is eaten by chickens.* (OV Agent)
> (Note that the '-ed' form becomes '-en' with this irregular verb.)

> *The maggot was swallowed by the fish.* (OV Agent)

Because this form is more complex and less common than the active voice, the passive is more difficult to process for inexperienced readers than the active, and its use may lead to comprehension difficulties. Using the passive gives the author the opportunity to put more emphasis on what would be the object in an active construction. It also allows the author to delete the agent of the action. In some texts, such as information books describing processes, the specific agent is relatively unimportant:

> *Bananas are cut when they are still green. They are packed in boxes and taken to sorting sheds, where the best bananas are selected and the rest rejected…*

However, this capacity to delete the agent can lead to some evasive writing. Compare:

> *The feeding of carrion to herbivores was legalised by the government during the 1980s.*
> *The feeding of carrion to herbivores was legalised during the 1980s.*

Given that it has been estimated that four out of five passive sentences in English omit the agent, it is important to remember that the use of the passive can provide opportunities for telling less than the whole story. Indeed, one could argue that in the banana farming example, it might be more informative to use active sentences in order to remind readers that these processes are carried out by long-suffering human beings.

● Although the section above provides only a cursory and simplified account of verb forms and functions, it is important to remember that all competent speakers of the English language have a thorough knowledge of its complexities. We can all produce and comprehend the range of aspects in the table on page 71; we can all detect and convey shades of meaning implied by the use of a range of modal auxiliaries; we can all appreciate the equivalence of meaning between active and passive forms.

The fact that our understanding of all this is implicit and automatic sometimes makes us forget just how complicated the body of knowledge we have mastered over a lifetime of using language is. Therefore, it may not be as easy to appreciate the difficulties that learners may encounter, particularly those who are acquiring English as an additional language. Irregular verb forms, the aspect system and the range of auxiliaries might appear daunting to such learners, so it is important to be reminded of their complexity.

● The tense system in English is particularly Byzantine, and even when children have mastered it in speech, it can take a while for such mastery to spread to their writing. Tense mixing is a feature with which every teacher will be familiar:

*My old house had a barbecue which we can cook **in**.*

*I couldn't get **no** supper because the supermarket is closed.*

Selecting the correct modal auxiliary to fit a conditional form is also a problem with quite mature writers:

*If the fire alarm **would** go off, you cannot run or shout.*

Awareness of the range of forms young writers have to decide between helps us to sympathise with their plight, and to think of ways of alleviating it.

● Another educational implication is the issue of subject–verb agreement. In standard English, the main verb or auxiliary changes its form according to the person and number of the subject. In some dialects, these verb forms remain unchanged. Traditionally, teachers would brand dialect forms as 'incorrect', and attempt to drill children in the standard forms through constant correction and pattern practices. Such approaches do not have an encouraging track record. It might make more sense to approach language variation in the spirit of investigation, acknowledging the greater consistency of dialect forms by making a systematic comparison with the standard pattern, as in the following table.

standard	dialect
I cook.	I cooks.
You cook.	You cooks.
She cooks.	She cooks.
We cook.	We cooks.
They cook.	They cooks.
I was cooking.	I was cooking.
You were cooking.	You was cooking.
She was cooking.	She was cooking.
We were cooking.	We was cooking.
They were cooking.	They was cooking.

All children should learn to use standard forms, while acknowledging that the investigation of dialectal variation can provide a rich source for learning about such forms.

● It is also important to realise that stylistic choices such as the use of the passive voice may create problems of comprehension for the inexperienced reader, and that it can be used by writers to bring forward information that they want to stress, or to delete information that they want to conceal.

Vocabulary

Aspect – the element of a verb referring to how the action of the verb should be regarded in terms of its completion or duration: *He **had eaten** already but **was contemplating** a second helping.* The two verbs in bold both refer to past time but differ aspectually.

Copular (linking verb) – a verb which links a subject to its complement, for example, *be, seem, appear, become, sound, feel, grow, turn* and *remain*.

Modifier – an element in a phrase occurring before or after the headword which adds to the meaning of that word: *The **gleaming** crockery **on the table** was immaculate.* The headword *crockery* in the subject noun phrase is premodified by the adjective *gleaming* and post-modified by the prepositional phrase *on the table*.

Passive – in a passive sentence the subject is the entity affected by the verb. The verb form changes and is accompanied by an auxiliary. In the following example, an active sentence is accompanied by its passive form: *The dog ate the meringue. The meringue was eaten by the dog.* Passive sentences allow the agent of the action to be omitted: *The meringue was eaten.*

Transitive/intransitive – transitive verbs require an object: *Fido enjoyed the meringue.* (The sentence would sound incomplete without the object.) Intransitive verbs do not require an object: *Fido growled.*

Amazing facts

The prize for irregularity goes to our most common verb, *be*, which in addition to its infinitive form has seven other realisations: the present tense *am, is* and *are*, the past tense *was* and *were*, the '-ing' form *being*, and the past participle *been*.

Common misconceptions

Some people believe that it is always wrong to split an infinitive (for example, *to boldly go*). This is another source of unnecessary pernicketiness arising from misconceived 18th century attempts to impose Latin norms on English. Infinitives are never split in Latin because in that language the infinitive is marked by a suffix (for example, *amare*, to love). Splitting a Latin infinitive would be like wedging an adverb between the stem and the suffix of an English participle (*goboldlying*). There is nothing wrong with putting an adverb between the *to* and the main word of an English infinitive as long as it does not disrupt the rhythm of the sentence. In some cases, putting the adverb elsewhere would sound odd. Compare:

*I think you're going to **jolly well** enjoy this dinner.*

*I think you're going **jolly well** to enjoy this dinner.*

When discussing this point with children, you should inform them that conservative opinion disapproves of the split infinitive, but you should also explain the mistaken, and relatively recent, source of this prejudice.

Teaching ideas

● Ask the children to identify and collect verb phrases from different types of text (for example, adventure stories, instructions and recipes, scientific description). Discuss how types of verb vary from text to text, contributing to the 'texture' of the genre. You could also ask them to predict what kinds of verbs are likely to occur in the material you present for shared reading, given the title and likely content.

● In order to highlight the function of a verb as the crux of the sentence (linking the subject to the rest of the sentence or, when standing alone with the subject, providing more information about it) give the children cloze procedures in which verb phrases have been deleted. Older children could prepare these for each other.

- Familiarise the children with the conventions of regular and irregular verb variation, in the course of daily shared writing. This is also a good way of modelling the use of irregular verbs to children who are still at the stage of 'overgeneralisation'. This term refers to the tendency of younger children to add '-ed' to past-tense forms regardless of the type of verb. For example, they will say *I thinked, I goed out, I sitted down* and so on. This tendency corrects itself in the course of primary schooling, but exposure to mature irregular forms through shared writing might help the process along.

- Shared writing is also a good way to highlight the importance of tense consistency. Once a story has been completed, the verbs can be highlighted and their past-tense forms noted. The pattern can be compared with the present-tense forms characteristic of a description, or you can experiment by retelling the story in the present historic:

> *It is midnight, and the mouse who crouches in the shadow of the kitchen table is unaware that a cat is approaching…*

While you do this, you will soon find that it is very difficult indeed to summarise ways in which verbs express time in any simple rules about tense patterns. For example, to say that we form the past tense by adding '-ed' to verbs would be a gross oversimplification. Asking children to spot different ways in which time is indicated is more likely to give them a feel for the anatomy of English.

- Explore subject–verb agreement by collecting examples of varying usage from the local speech community, from literature and the media. Constructing comparison tables like the one given on page 74 can be a useful task for older children (but it can also be a dry and confusing exercise if it is done as a worksheet activity not grounded in active research and discussion). Try to resist the temptation to label non-standard forms as incorrect. Regional and social class dialects have as respectable a pedigree as standard English, and even from a pragmatic point of view, you are unlikely to persuade children to use standard forms by labelling their home languages as defective.

● Demonstrate the role of auxiliaries by asking the children to start with a sentence using a lone main verb in the verb phrase slot, and to see how its meaning changes as the verb phrase is expanded and modulated:

> My cat **hunts** mice.
> My cat **can hunt** mice.
> My cat **might hunt** mice.
> My cat **might have hunted** mice.
> My cat **might have been hunting** mice.

Encourage the children to identify a context for each of the sentences, and to note how the inflection of the main verb changes with the auxiliaries.

● Examine the use of the passive voice by looking at texts in which it occurs frequently (usually non-fiction passages describing or reporting on processes). Older children can be shown how the passive allows an impersonal tone in such texts. Ask them to rewrite short active texts in the passive, and to note the effects; they may also 'translate' passive texts into the active voice, inserting active subjects where necessary. The use of the passive to delete or conceal agency should be pointed out (historical texts and contemporary journalism are good sources) but the best way to introduce this feature is with examples of its use in everyday speech:

> Mum, the toast's been burned.

Adjectives

Subject facts

Traditionally, adjectives have been defined as describing words or, more precisely, words which modify or tell us more about nouns. This is a good enough start, but as we have already seen there are many noun-modifying words which are not formally adjectives.

Adjectives are used to add detail to accounts and to specify the qualities of nouns. They can occur in noun phrases before the noun, either singly, in series, or as part of an adjective phrase containing an intensifying or qualifying adverb:

> We bought a kilo of **black** grapes.
> We bought a kilo of **juicy, fragrant black** grapes.
> We bought a kilo of **intensely vinous black** grapes.
> We bought a kilo of **somewhat expensive black** grapes.

Theoretically, any number of adjectives can precede a noun, but using too many overloads the sentence and creates a highly unnatural style.

It is interesting to note that the order in which adjectives occur is subject to some restriction:

> a bunch of lovely, big, black Greek grapes

sounds fine, but there is something slightly odd about
> a bunch of Greek, black, big, lovely grapes

Deriving the rules for 'acceptable' sequences can be a stimulating investigation.

As well as preceding nouns, adjectives can also occur after certain verbs as subject or object complements. Again, they can appear in this position either singly, in a series or as part of a phrase.

---

subject complements
The grapes looked *delectable*.
The grapes smelled *sharp and refreshing*.
The grapes tasted *excruciatingly bitter*.

object complements
I considered the grapes *extravagant*.
Giles declared the grapes *peerless and perfect*.
Rebecca thought the grapes *rather disappointing*.

In this position, the adjectival phrase can contain a prepositional phrase:

*The grapes tasted **more delightful with cheese**.*

*We found the grapes **prone to rapid fermentation**.*

When an adjective occurs before a noun, this is referred to as the attributive function. When it occurs as a complement, this is referred to as its predicative function. It has been suggested that one of the differences between spoken and written language is that in the former adjectives are more commonly used predicatively, while in the latter they are more commonly used attributively. Compare:

This peach is lovely and juicy.
(spoken language, predicative function)

A plump, juicy peach was hanging on the bough.
(written language, attributive function)

This is by no means a hard and fast distinction, though it might be borne in mind by teachers trying to persuade children to 'use more adjectives', when the intention is usually to promote the attributive role. It is not, of course, unusual to find attributive adjectives in spoken language, though attributive adjective chains in this mode sometimes represent an attempt at a 'literary' effect:

*Some **big, fat, dirty, stinking, greedy** glutton has been at my packed lunch!*

***Lovely, juicy, sweet** satsumas going for a pound a bag!*

Adjectives as nouns
Some adjectives, usually referring to groups of people, can act as nouns:

*The **Dutch** first mastered the art of mingling fruit and beer.*

*We honour the **rich** and punish the **poor**.*

In certain set noun phrases, adjectives follow rather than precede nouns:

*the siege **perilous***

spaghetti **bolognese**
persons **unknown**
rhesus **negative**

Comparisons

Most adjectives are 'gradable', and can therefore be used to express comparisons by adding the inflections '-er' and '-est' or the words *more* and *most*. Monosyllabic adjectives generally take the inflections:

*Maple syrup is **sweeter** than honey, but the juice of these grapes is the **sweetest** liquid I've ever supped.*

Other adjectives, particularly those that are polysyllabic, take the words *more* or *most*:

*Mineral water is **more refreshing** than champagne, but the juice of these grapes is the **most refreshing** liquid I've ever swallowed.*

Gradable adjectives can also be compared to a lower degree by using the words *less* and *least*:

*These melons are **less sweet** than those kumquats, but these grapes are the **least sweet** of any fruit I've ever tasted.*

And they can be compared to the same degree by using the construction *as…as*.

*These grapes are **as dear as** diamonds.*

Many adjectives, however, are not gradable. We can describe somebody as an *utter* glutton, but it would sound wrong to describe his greedier friend as being an *uttererer* glutton, or a *very utter* glutton, or a *more utter* glutton. (However, we could call somebody the *uttermost* glutton I've ever met.)

A small class of adjectives, by their very meaning, defy both comparison and qualification because they express ultimate qualities. These include *infinite, eternal, unique* and *ultimate* itself. Therefore, from a conservative point of view, phrases such as *most unique* are incorrect.

Adjective endings

Although many adjectives lack distinctive endings, a common one in everyday adjectives is '-y' (*merry, silly, happy, cosy* and so on.) This feature is often added facetiously to other types of words in order to invent a convenient adjective:

*I've had a bit of a **snacky** diet since catching the flu.*

More formally, '-y' is one of the many suffixes that can be added to nouns or verbs in order to form adjectives. Examples of this and other adjective-forming suffixes can be found in the following tables:

leaf	leafy
string	stringy
shake	shaky

freeze	-able	freezable
fancy	-ful	fanciful
part	-ial	partial
peck	-ish	peckish
skin	-less	skinless
love	-ly	lovely
odour	-ous	odorous
sea	-worthy	seaworthy

Note how the addition of these suffixes can cause changes to the spelling of the stem. Sometimes the spelling change can be quite drastic, obscuring the derivation of the adjective.

beast	bestial
feast	festive
star	stellar

● Adjectives are one of the three word classes most often talked about in primary classrooms, the others being nouns and verbs.

● The form and functions of the class of adjectives appears to be quite straightforward, but you might find it interesting to consider some of their less obvious complexities.

Teaching ideas

● Children are often asked to underline adjectives in pieces of text and to insert adjectives into passages which lack them. Presumably the point of the first exercise is to teach children what adjectives are, and of the second to encourage their use. It is worth bearing in mind, however, that only children who can already recognise adjectives are going to succeed at the first task, while the second task assumes that a text filled with adjectives is necessarily better than one without. An overemphasis on the use of adjectives is evident in the common response that children give when they are asked how they might improve their writing: 'Use more adjectives.'

This can often lead to the production of writing which feels stiff and stuffed, especially in instances when the text is the product of such an exercise:

The hot, liquid soup was poured into the round, blue, china bowls.

The cuboidal, brown loaf was sliced into thick, rectangular slices with a long, sharp stainless-steel knife.

Fortunately, this artificial overuse of attributive adjectives rarely transfers to children's spontaneous writing.

● As an alternative way of encouraging children to consider the usefulness of adjectives, help them to compare texts representing different 'richnesses' of usage. Ask accomplished writers to create texts which overuse adjectives, so that their classmates can be helped to identify those that are effective and to edit out redundant ones; encourage them to search thesauruses to find synonyms for overworked adjectives. Older children can try to find 'plain English' equivalents for pretentiously exotic adjectives. The objective should be to strike a balance between appreciating clever use of an expanding vocabulary and demonstrating restraint and clarity.

● Familiarise younger children with the use of adjectives by letting them examine objects by touch, visually and by smell. Discuss their responses and write the words they have used on a chart, with columns for texture, shape, size, colour and so on. Collect phrases as well as words. Ask the children if they can think of other objects, beings and situations that selected words and phrases could be applied to. Charts can then be made to show how adjectives can have metaphorical as well as literal applications.

● Discuss with the children the common prejudice against the word *nice*. Brainstorm alternatives to this adjective, perhaps using a chart like the one below:

Synonyms for nice		
food	**people**	**music**
flavourful	kind	soothing
delicious	considerable	exhilarating
nourishing	generous	melodious
refreshing	modest	harmonious

However, suggest that there are contexts in which this humble word is indispensable:

This is a nice cup of tea. Not spectacular, just nice.

● Young children are often fascinated by dissonances and mismatches which result in nonsense. A simple way to harness this interest, while helping the children to learn about adjectives, is to play a game in which children draw two cards, one from an adjective deck and the other from a noun deck. Ensure beforehand that the combinations are likely to create bizarre phrases, for example *square sausage, sharp sandwich, spiky supper, slithery sardine*. The children can then draw the objects denoted.

● Examine the role of adjectives in media such as advertising and song lyrics. Instead of getting children to underline all the adjectives in arbitrary texts, ask them to underline all the adjectives in specific genres of advertising – fashion, health or sports magazines, for example – to highlight the way in which language can be used to persuade and manipulate.

● Play simple card games to show the relationships between adjectives and nouns. For example, prepare a set of cards with a noun on one side and related adjectives on the other. Spread the cards out in front of the children with the adjectives showing but not the nouns. Ask the children to guess what the words on the other side of the cards are likely to be. When they have had a few goes at this, show them how to write their own cards on a particular theme

Side 1	Side 2
cold	
hard	ice
slippery	
windy	
violent	hurricane
destructive	
warm	
bright	sunlight
pleasant	

● Older children are often fascinated by the way in which oral language changes, and adjectives are at the forefront of such change. Start by talking to the whole class about what words they currently use as expressions of admiration (such words change with bewildering rapidity). Tell the class about equivalent terms used when you were their age (*wicked, ace, brill?*). Derogatory adjectives can also be explored – an interesting phenomenon is the use of nouns denoting articles of clothing as derogatory adjectives:

You press wild flowers? That's really anorak.

I don't go there. It's absolutely pants.

Use the discussion to launch investigations in which children explore textual material to research examples of changing usage. For example, relatively recent changes like the extension in the meaning of *industrial* (industrial action) and the 'trivialisation' of *wicked* and *awesome*, can be compared with long-term changes such as the shift in meaning *silly* and *sophisticated*. (*Silly*, derived from Anglo-Saxon *saelig*, originally meant 'blessed' or 'saintly' – as the current German *selig* does. In Chaucer and Shakespeare it was used in the sense of innocent and simple, from which the connotation 'simple-mindedness' or 'stupidity' arose. *Sophisticated* originates from *sophistry* – the art of deceptive but plausible reasoning; hence its earlier connotations of 'clever trickery'.)

Regional variations in dialect can also feed into the investigation: children can collect examples of adjectives such as *mardy, mockadawed* and *lathered*, and assess the extent to which they are still used in the local community.

● Choices of adjective according to the connotations that words carry is also an important area. Display a chart similar to the one below and invite the children to discuss possibilities for filling in the gaps and extending it:

I enjoy eating. I am…	greedy	appreciative
I enjoy talking. I am…	talkative	sociable
I like studying. I am…	dorky	studious
My house is tiny. It is…	poky	
Oscar doesn't talk much. He is…	reserved	

Talk to the children about the factors that would determine which choice of word a person might make, and discuss how similar choices made by people such as journalists, broadcasters and editors could affect the way in which we view people and events.

● On a more formal level, children can investigate the structure and derivation of adjectives by combining nouns and verbs with adjective-making suffixes, using a table like the one shown above. New adjectives can be coined for particular purposes by making novel combinations: .

The nishnickety noise of personal stereos makes me murderous.

Have a sparkling glass of our new fizzivivish health drink.

Adverbs

Subject facts

The adverb word class has sometimes been called the 'dustbin' class because it contains words that perform a wide variety of functions which do not fit neatly into any other category.

The most familiar function of adverbs and adverb phrases is to provide further information about the verb in a sentence. As such they often occupy the adverbial element in clause structure, specifying such aspects as manner, time and place.

*We dined **slowly**.*
*We dined **very late indeed**.*
*We dined **outside**.*

Adverbs can also occur within phrases to modify adjectives, intensifying or 'diminishing' them:

*They do an **extremely** nutritious muesli for breakfast here.*

*The taste and texture are **absolutely** fabulous.*

*The so-called hotpot was **scarcely** warm.*

*I became **somewhat** angry at this.*

They can also perform the same role with other adverbs:

*I complained **very** bitterly about the hot-pot.*

*The waiter responded **rather** arrogantly.*

These adverbs are often called degree adverbs; other examples are *almost, barely, entirely, highly, quite, slightly, totally* and *utterly.*

As we have seen, adverbs are used to modify verbs, adjectives and other adverbs. Normally, they cannot be used to modify nouns, but in some informal contexts they may precede nouns when the noun is being used in a facetiously adjectival way:

*This pub is **very** Coronation Street.*

*If you want a **really** Shangri-La experience, look no further.*

Another important class of adverb, sometimes called conjuncts or connectives, is used to join sentences, contributing to the connectivity or coherence of a text:

*My dinner was ruined. **Consequently** I resorted to the chip shop.*

*The chippy was closed. **However**, the kebab shop was open.*

Yet another type of adverb provides a commentary on a whole sentence:

***Frankly**, I do enjoy a well-stuffed pouch of pitta bread.*

***Hopefully**, I won't regret it in the morning.*

(Some language conservatives argue that *hopefully* should only be used to modify verbs, not sentences.)

Many adverbs can be formed from adjectives by adding an '-ly' ending:

adjective	adverb
warm	warmly
sweet	sweetly
skilful	skilfully
sudden	suddenly
strange	strangely

Other adverb-forming suffixes include '-wise' (*clockwise*), '-wards' (*eastwards*) and '-ways' (*sideways*).

Note that the '-ly' ending does not imply that a word is an adverb, because many adjectives end in this way as well:

*Iris is a **kindly**, **friendly** and **lively** hostess who prepares **costly** but **deadly** meals.*

Many words can be used either as adjectives or adverbs, depending on whether they modify a noun or a verb:

*We ate very **early**.* (adv)
*We had an **early** breakfast.* (adj)

*I will be arriving **late**.* (adv)
*I caught a **late** train.* (adj)

*I bake bread **daily**.* (adv)
*Give us this day our **daily** bread.* (adj)

*He works **hard** all night.* (adv: *work* is an verb)
*This is really **hard** work.* (adj: *work* is a noun)

*Run **fast**!* (adv)
*The **fast** train might just get you there on time.* (adj)

Why you need to know these facts

● Children are often taught that adverbs are words that end in '-ly' and that they tell us more about verbs. As we have seen, the picture is a bit more complicated than this. It is important to be clear about the diverse forms that adverbs can take and the variety of functions that they can serve. Although oversimplification regarding this complex and diverse word class is unlikely to be lethal to a child's language development, it can lead to avoidable confusion.

● More significantly, knowledge of the role played by sentence adverbs in contributing to the logical structure of different types of written language can help you to be more aware of text difficulty and of the learner's ability to comprehend and produce formal writing. Comprehension studies have shown that many readers have great difficulty in appreciating the logical relations signalled by such words as *accordingly, consequently, furthermore, hence, moreover, similarly* and *therefore*. These words are rare in informal speech, but common in non-fiction texts and absolutely crucial to the structure of ideas within such texts. Accordingly, it is perfectly possible to understand the content of individual sentences within a passage but to miss the point of the passage as a whole because of haziness regarding these connective adverbs. Ensuring that children can understand such terms and deploy them in their own writing is essential to the mastery of a variety of important types of prose.

Teaching ideas

● Ask the children to look at how adverbs are used in texts such as sports reports and newscasts. This will illustrate how adverbs are used to modify verbs:

> Norkovitch **deftly** executes *a semi-spandrel on the radial beam,* **swiftly and gracefully** *transforming this move into an* **extremely** *adventurous triple fish-tail…*

Then, in their own writing, they can play with the effects of inserting adverb phrases into different sentence slots:

> The cat approached the goldfish bowl **slowly and stealthily**.
> The cat, **slowly and stealthily**, approached the goldfish bowl.
> **Slowly and stealthily**, the cat approached the goldfish bowl.

● Give the children a popular wordplay activity which involves linking verbs with '-ly' adverbs that are related in humorous ways:

> Dobbin neighed hoarsely.
>
> The milkman yawned mournfully.
>
> The kayak capsized rapidly.

● Practise the use of sentence adverbs through a variety of oral text creation games. 'Fortunately/unfortunately' is a useful starting-point. This involves telling the children a short story of your own invention in which alternate sentences after the opening one begin with *fortunately* and *unfortunately*.

> On my way to work this morning I was attacked by a Rottweiler. **Fortunately**, the owner was a friend of mine and told the dog to behave. **Unfortunately**, it took no notice of her. **Fortunately**, I was carrying my electronic dog frightener in my bag. **Unfortunately**, the batteries had run down and it didn't work…

Once the children are clear about how the two connective terms work, provide a starter sentence for another story and ask them to contribute a sentence at a time in completing it.

Then introduce other types of connective. Explain to the children that there are a wide range of words and phrases that act as signals between sentences, indicating how what is to come relates to what has just been said. This is best put across by demonstration:

> When I was on my way to work this morning I was attacked by a Rottweiler. **However**, it was only a small Rottweiler, and I was able to scare it off by pulling a fierce face. **Furthermore**, I am so good at pulling fierce faces that I could have frightened a much larger animal. **Suddenly**…

Word classes and phrase types

● Having introduced children to these words through oral activity and narrative, their functions in non-fiction can be explored. A useful strategy is to provide children with frames in which sentences cued by different types of sentence adverb must be completed appropriately:

> *Squanto saved the Pilgrim Fathers from starvation.*
> *Accordingly…*
> *Squanto saved the Pilgrim Fathers from starvation.*
> *Consequently…*
> *Squanto saved the Pilgrim Fathers from starvation.*
> *However…*

It is of course vital that the children have been familiarised through their reading with how these words are used before they can be expected to deploy them in writing.

Prepositions

Subject facts

As the word suggests, prepositions go in front of other words and phrases to signal a relationship between elements in a sentence. Often, but not always, this is a relationship of place:

> *I'll meet you **at** the Pie and Mash **in** the Old Kent Road.*

They can also show relationships of time:

> *Be there **before** two o'clock.*

Of cause:

> *I was late **because** of the traffic.*

And of manner:

> *I ate my pie **with** relish and mustard.*

92 The Primary Teacher's Guide to Grammar and Punctuation

A single preposition can fulfil a variety of functions:

> I arrived **at** ten past.
> I was **at** the bus stop for an hour.
> I'm no good **at** being punctual.
> I got really angry **at** the driver.

Prepositions can consist of one, two or three words:

> It's **about** time we left.
> It's **close to** midnight.
> I've parked **in front of** the bus shelter.

Prepositions usually precede noun phrases or pronouns:

> I looked **through** the window.
> I strode **into** the pie shop.
> I sat down **next to** him.

Less frequently, they precede adjectives, adverbs and clauses:

> You've arrived **at** last.
> **In** brief, I'm famished.
> The gravy is better **by** far.
> Let's go **to** the place we went to last time.

Sometimes prepositions can be 'stranded' or separated from the noun to which they relate:

> This is the pie I've been dreaming **about.**
> Which cup have you been drinking **from?**
> She's the girl I was talking **to** last Saturday.

(Remember that there is nothing ungrammatical about the placing of the prepositions in the first two examples above.)

A prepositional phrase consists of a preposition together with the string of words, usually a noun phrase, that follows it. Prepositional phrases can act as the adverbial element within clauses:

> He leaned **against the window.**

>*She sat **on the table**.*
>*They gazed **through the rain-streaked glass**.*

They can also form parts of noun phrases, post-modifying the head noun:

>*The girl **behind the counter** looked bored.*
>*He selected the pie **with the palest crust**.*
>*She gave me a cup **without a handle**.*

The noun phrase following a preposition can itself be modified by another prepositional phrase, a process that could, theoretically, be continued indefinitely:

>*I spoke to the girl **with the scowl behind the counter in the pie shop on the corner of Old Kent Road on Saturday last week**.*

Many prepositional phrases have figurative meanings. In the following example, none of the prepositional phrases can be interpreted in a literal sense:

>*That chef is **up the wall**. He'll end up **in hot water** if he carries on like that. Perhaps he's feeling **under the weather**, or maybe his job is **on the line**. I hope he's **over the worst** of it now.*

These phrases are examples of idioms: the separate words combine to form a single meaning that is not derivable from their individual meanings. Idioms are formulaic – that is, we cannot tinker with their component parts; it would be senseless, for example, to say that somebody is *under the best* of it.

Why you need to know these facts

● As adults, we command the several dozen prepositions of English and their many functions easily and unconsciously, but this is not as easy for less-experienced language users. The rules governing preposition usage can be puzzling for children learning to speak and for all people acquiring English as an additional language. A major problem is that the same verb can take different prepositions according to the noun phrase that follows it, even if these noun phrases seem to have very similar roles. The noun phrases in the following examples all relate to location, but take different prepositions:

> We arrived **at** the barbecue.
> We arrived **in** Liverpool.
> We arrived **on** the tarmac.

Confusions arising from this are common in the speech of young children and non-native speakers:

> I can swim **inside** the water now.
> I've been waiting **until** three hours for you.
> In winter I wear a vest **below** my shirt.

Older children who are beginning to try out sophisticated structures in their writing can also encounter difficulties with prepositions:

> The container **in which** the spores are found **in** is called the sporangium.

It is important to understand that such errors are signs of growth; teachers should be aware of the complexities being attempted, and should commend the learner for the attempt as well as showing them how to use the correct structure.

Amazing facts

The 'rule' about never ending a sentence with a preposition is said to have been invented by John Dryden in the 17th century. Before then, nobody saw anything wrong with the practice. Explaining this to children might help them to understand how language can be influenced by the prejudices of individuals and groups. Beware of the oversimplification that a preposition answers the question 'Where?' As we have seen, these words perform a variety of roles within sentences, of which the indication of position is only one.

Teaching ideas

● Young children who are learning English as their first language will learn to sort out the prepositional system without explicit instruction. If children who are learning English as an additional language are having difficulties, an audit should be made of the structures they find difficult, and particular attention paid to these in the course of shared writing. Composing 'prepositional stories' along the lines of *Rosie's Walk* by Pat Hutchins (Red Fox) or *There's a Wocket in my Pocket!* by Dr Seuss (Collins Beginner Books) may provide more focused input.

● Children might also be interested in collecting idiomatic prepositional phrases and seeing how many of them they can fit into a short story of, say, 200 words.

● Ask the children to try to make up their own prepositional idioms. Possibilities might include:

| over the moon | on target |
| against the grain | behind time |

Conjunctions

Subject facts

Conjunctions are used to join grammatical elements together in various ways. The simplest conjunctions are coordinators, which join together elements of equal importance. The most common coordinators are *and, but* and *or.* They can be used to join phrases consisting of one or more words:

*Our <u>Mother **and** Child</u> Reunion Special consists of <u>chicken **and** eggs</u>.*

*The use of spices in Punjabi cooking is <u>subtle **but** decisive</u>.*

*You can fry the scrapple <u>quickly **or** slowly</u>.*

*All meals come with <u>six oven-baked potato cakes **and** home-made salad dressing</u>.*

*A good stir-fry needs to be executed <u>quite carefully **but** very quickly indeed</u>.*

*Do you like your cider <u>dry as sand **or** sweet as syllabub</u>?*

And they can be used to join clauses of equal 'weight' in order to make compound sentences:

*Cherice chose the scrumpy **and** I had the perry.*

*Scrapple is a lethal substance **but** it warms the cockles of your heart.*

*You can eat your potato cakes **or** you can give them to me.*

Using *and*

This appears to be simple but there are hidden complexities in the uses of coordinators, particularly *and*, the most common example. Normally, except in formulaic phrases such as *fish and chips, slow but steady, hell or high water*, the order in which the joined items, or conjoins, occur is unimportant. Consider, however, the range of uses to which *and* can be put. If it expresses simultaneous action, the order of conjoins is irrelevant:

*Emily peeled the potatoes **and** Luke cracked the coconuts.*

Nor does it matter if the conjunction is between phrases that express additional meaning:

*By the time the meal was ready Emily had peeled her thumb **and** Luke had cracked two fingers.*

However, *and* can provide both a timeline and a sense of 'cause and effect', in which the order of conjunctions is fixed:

*Emily was weeping **and** I felt sorry for her.*

Subordinating conjunctions

Subordinating conjunctions are used in complex sentences where a main clause includes or is accompanied by clauses which depend on the main clause. These subordinate or dependent clauses can be linked to this main clause by a variety of subordinating conjunctions. The choice of subordinator, which can consist of more than one word, indicates the relationship between the main and dependent clauses:

*We went fishing **because** we were hungry.*
*We went fishing **when** the moon rose.*
*We went fishing **assuming that** we'd be having trout for breakfast.*

In compound sentences, the conjunction has to come between the linked elements, but in complex sentences the conjunction is more mobile because the dependent clause it precedes can be placed before, after or inside the main clause:

***Although it was raining**, the boys went out in the fishing boat.*
*The boys went out in the fishing boat, **so that they could fill the freezer**.*
*The boys, **who should have known better**, went out in the fishing boat.*

The most common subordinating conjunctions are *after, although, as, because, before, if, once, since, that, though, unless, until, when, where* and *while*.

Why you need to know these facts

● Conjunctions are important elements in building texts. Though the use of coordinating conjunctions appears relatively straightforward there are, as we have seen, some complexities involved. The use of subordinating conjunctions is inseparable from a consideration of complex sentences, which will be dealt with in the next chapter.

Vocabulary

Complex sentence – a sentence consisting of a main clause accompanied by one or more clauses which are dependent upon the main clause: *She kneaded the dough* **because she needed the dough**. The clause in bold in this complex sentence depends for its meaning on the initial clause.

Compound sentence – a sentence consisting of two or more coordinated main clauses.

Amazing facts

One of the sillier challenges in linguistics is to concoct sentences in which a syllable can be consecutively repeated as many times as possible without creating nonsense (for example, *In order to get to Arbroath, take the A4 for Forfar for four miles*). One of the candidates is the remark made by a passer-by to a sign-writer who had just repainted the title of a firm known as Welland and Anderson: *You've left too much space between* **Well** *and* **-and** *and* **-and** *and* **and** *and* **and** *and* **And** *and* **And** *and* **-erson**.

Common misconceptions

The fallacy that one must never begin a sentence with *and, but* or *because* (see Chapter 1, pages 12–13) is still widespread. As long ago as 1951, Sir Ernest Gowers, consultant to the Treasury on the improvement of official English (and author of *The Complete Plain Words*, Penguin) stated that there were no grounds for this prejudice, yet it has proved very tenacious and is still repeated as a matter of fact in classrooms throughout the land.

Teaching ideas

● Ask the children to brainstorm short statements (on a current topic) and use appropriate conjunctions to link the statements into more economical texts. In many cases, changes other than the insertion of conjunctions will be necessary. Start with pairs of sentences. For example:

Bread is a very common foodstuff. It comes in many different forms.

can become:

Bread is a very common foodstuff and comes in many different forms.

or:

Bread is a very common foodstuff which comes in many different forms.

Similarly, several sentences can be linked together to make one or two sentences:

Butter is made by churning milk. It is a very fatty substance. It is spread on bread. It tastes lovely. It is full of calories. It is high in cholesterol.

This can be turned into:

Butter is a very fatty substance which is made by churning milk. It is spread on bread and tastes lovely, but it is full of calories and high in cholesterol.

● Help the children to complete complex sentences from which the words following the subordinator have been deleted. This will enable them to practise the use of subordinating conjunctions:

Because _____ , the tea shop was a very welcome sight.

You can't come in here unless _____.

My friend, who _____ , wasn't very pleased.

Looking at short texts from which conjunctions have been deleted and inviting children to reinsert them can also be a useful activity, but only if it is done occasionally, cooperatively and with a text that will be enjoyable to read once it has been reconstructed.

Resources

What's in a Word? by Norah McWilliam (Trentham Books) provides a rich set of resources and ideas for investigating words, with an emphasis on the multilingual classroom.

The best resource is as wide a variety as you can accumulate of texts of different kinds illustrating the forms and functions of words. These should include newspapers, comics and magazines, junk mail, advertisements, notices, jokes, word games and texts from earlier generations.

A good collection of dictionaries and wordbooks should also be available in the classroom.

Compound and complex sentences

Chapters 1 and 2 of this book have considered mainly simple sentences. Much of the textual richness of writing depends on the variety of structures used by writers deploying the seven basic clause types. However, a great deal depends on the fact that we are able to combine these basic building blocks into more involved structures, either by linking clauses of equal status into compound sentences (the process of coordination) or by embedding clauses of lesser status into main clauses in order to make complex sentences (the process of subordination).

Compound sentences

Subject facts

We saw in the section on clauses (see pages 20–26) that simple sentences contain only one clause:

I was hungry.
The food was making my mouth water.
The band was making an atrocious noise.

We can, however, join clauses up to make longer and more complicated sentences:

I was hungry and the food was making my mouth water but the band was making an atrocious noise.

Compound and complex sentences

Sentences in which two or more clauses of equal 'weight' are joined up are known as compound sentences, and the process of joining them is called coordination. Frequently, a joining word, which is called a coordinating conjunction or coordinator, is used to join the clauses, though it is also possible to use commas if the relationship between the separate clauses is simply one of addition:

> *The food was spicy, the conversation was spicier, the company was spiciest of all.*

Another way of joining equally important clauses is to use a semicolon (see page 129). Note how this has a more decisive effect than the use of the comma:

> *I have never eaten a better rabbit in my life;*
> *I have never eaten a worse crumble.*

The three main coordinators are *and*, *or* and *but*:

> *The main course was rabbit **and** the dessert was apple crumble.*

> *You can put up with the music **or** go hungry.*

> *I ate my dinner **but** the band almost spoiled it for me.*

Note that the second example shows how some clause elements can be omitted from a compound sentence. In this case, there is no need to repeat *you can* in the second clause. The process of omission is known as ellipsis, and the 'missing' element is said to have been elided or ellipted. As well as eliding subjects, verbs and objects can also be elided in compound sentences:

> *I cooked for ten guests but [ ] served only six [ ].*

Sometimes the elision can occur in the first clause:

> *Agnes was slicing [ ] and Jonquil buttering the bread.*

Another important process in compound sentences is that of substitution, where a pro-form takes the place of a word or phrase used earlier, in order to avoid repetition:

*I sought out the wine waiter and congratulated **him**.*

*Freya helped herself to port and Josie had **some** too.*

*I prefer Madeira and so **does** Alfred.*

*Phoebe is under the table and Frank is **there** too.*

Why you need to know these facts

● Children's early writing often consists of a stream of coordinated clauses, often not divided into manageable chunks:

We went to the beach and we had a picnic and I ate three sausage rolls and one was full of sand and I went for a swim and my little sister got pinched by a crab…

An awareness of the processes by which this kind of writing can be structured into more coherent sequences of compound (and complex) sentences can help you to develop a child's writing style.

Vocabulary

Ellipsis – the omission of words, phrases or clauses from sentences in the interests of coherence and economy. The ellipted (or elided) elements can be derived from the context: *Is that Holly's meringue? No, it's Oliver's…*
Coordinate clause – a clause forming a part of a compound sentence in conjunction with one or more clauses of equal status.

Teaching ideas

● Present the children with examples of coordinated clause chains like the one above. Explore ways of restructuring the writing into simple compound and complex sentences.

● In the course of shared writing, look at alternative ways
in which substitution, ellipsis and the use of conjunctions and
punctuation can be used to join sentences:

We were cold. We were tired. We were hungry.
We were cold and tired and hungry.
We were cold, tired and hungry.

● Show how substitution and ellipsis work to avoid repetition by
presenting texts in which these processes are absent and helping
the children to simplify them:

The soup and the toast came to the table late. The soup was
cold and the toast was cold. I called over the manager and asked
the manager why the soup was cold and the toast was cold.
The manager agreed that the soup was cold and the toast was
cold but claimed that the soup was cold and the toast was cold
because in the manager's country it was the custom…

In the above example, the first two sentences can be combined
into *The soup and the toast came to the table late and were cold,*
demonstrating how ellipsis reduces unnatural repetition.

Complex sentences

Subject facts

In complex sentences, a main clause is accompanied by a clause
of lesser weight, which is known as a subordinate or dependent
clause. Subordinate clauses can either express a complete clause
element, or they can be tucked away inside other constructions
which are acting as the clause element:

*I realised **that the custard had gone cold**.*

*The rum sauce **which had been simmering on the stove** burst*
into flames.

In the first example, the subordinate clause *that the custard had gone cold* is acting as the object clause element. In the second sentence, the subordinate clause *which had been simmering on the stove* is tucked inside the noun phrase *the rum sauce which had been simmering on the stove*, and it is this entire noun phrase that is acting as the subject clause element.

Just as subjects, objects and complements can be realised by noun phrases, they can also be realised by nominal clauses – that is, by subordinate clauses which have the force of noun phrases. In the following examples, the bold nominal clauses are acting as subject, object, subject complement and object complement respectively:

> *Why the band continued to play was a great mystery.* (subject)

> *Lydia said that the quality of the music turned her soup sour.* (object)

> *The most amazing thing about the evening was that we all have happy memories of it.* (subject complement)

> *You can think of this whatever you like.* (object complement)

Non-finite nominal clauses (see page 24) can also act as clause elements:

> *Eating in that atmosphere was very courageous.*

> *I expected to wake up with indigestion.*

> *The plan was to leave before midnight.*

> *I found the wine waiter to be a very cool customer.*

The adverbial clause element is often realised by an adverbial clause of time, reason (or cause), result, condition, purpose, concession, location and manner. The following sentences show an example of each:

> *I left the restaurant when the dawn chorus was in full throat.* (time)

I was exhausted **because I had been laughing for hours**. (reason)

I felt very thirsty **so I bought a coffee at the taxi stand**. (result)

If it had tasted good, *I would have bought another one*. (condition)

I drank it slowly **so that I wouldn't scald my throat**. (purpose)

Although it was comforting, *it didn't quench my thirst*. (concession)

I left my hat **where the taxi drivers hang their coats**. (location)

I walked home quickly **as I usually do in the afternoon**. (manner)

The adverbial can also be expressed by a non-finite adverbial clause. The following examples show non-finite adverbial clauses of time, reason, purpose and concession:

Having finished off the port, *we started on the brandy*. (time)

Being a teetotaller, *Patrick drank tomato juice all night*. (reason)

I joined the guests under the table **to be sociable**. (purpose)

Though ridiculed by every diner, *the band played doggedly on*. (concession)

The choice of subordinating conjunction, which may consist of more than one word, shows the relationship between the main and the subordinate clauses:

I put up with the band **because** *I was so hungry*.

I enjoyed the rabbit **although** *I'm usually intolerant to meat*.

I left **before** *the band stopped playing*.

Whereas the positions of coordinated clauses are fixed in relation to each other, subordinate clauses can come before or after the main clause, or they can be set within the main clause:

> *Although it was made with splendid Bramleys*, the crumble was practically inedible.
>
> The trombone player, **who should have known better**, tried to sing and play at the same time.

Subordinate clauses that are linked to the main clause with words such as *who, what, which, what* and *that* are known as relative clauses, and these subordinating words as relative pronouns (see page 57). Relative clauses are of two types: restrictive (or defining) and non-restrictive (or non-defining).

A restrictive relative clause is used to identify which particular thing or idea is the topic of the sentence:

> *The violinist who finished off my crumble later died.* (restrictive)
> *The violinist, who finished off my crumble, later died.*
> (non-restrictive)

In the first example, the relative clause is restrictive. It is implied that there was more than one violinist, but only the one who finished off the crumble died. In the second example, the relative clause is non-restrictive. The sentence implies that there was only one violinist, and the relative clause adds optional extra information about him. Note that the use of commas around the non-restrictive relative clause serves the essential role of removing the ambiguity that would be conveyed by the words alone.

Finally, it is possible to combine coordinated and subordinated clauses into compound-complex or complex-compound sentences:

> *Although* the food was good **and** the company was cheerful, there was something strange about that night.

> I won't go there again **unless** they improve the crumble **or** sack the band.

Why you need to know these facts

● The writing of young children is often characterised by chains of clauses coordinated with a repetitive *and*. It is useful to know what other options are available. Subordination is a more complex process than coordination, and develops later in both speech and writing. It is useful to know what is involved in achieving this, and to look out for signs of this development. Very often children will make mistakes when they begin to try out these more complex sentence structures:

> *The Romans who travelled from their sunny home countries all the way to Britain was too cold for them.*

Here the child has used a long and ambitious restrictive relative clause to make the sentence more informative. In doing this, she has made the understandable error of leaving out a chunk from the main clause (which was probably intended to be something like *The Romans found that this country was too cold for them*).

It is important to see such errors as signs of growth, and to welcome the initial achievement that they signal, rather than branding them as careless.

Vocabulary

Relative clause – a subordinate clause which either provides optional information about a preceding noun phrase (a non-restrictive or non-defining relative clause), or which restricts the reference of the main clause to that particular noun phrase (a restrictive or defining relative clause). *My brother, **who lives in Kingston**, is a mushroom expert.* (Non-restrictive.) *My brother **who lives in Kingston** is a mushroom expert.* (Restrictive.)

Teaching ideas

● Take a simple sentence such as *My sister likes crumble* and see how many ways the children can expand it using words, phrases and clauses:

> *After she's eaten her dinner, my sister likes crumble.*
> *My sister, who has a sweet tooth, likes crumble.*
> *My sister likes crumble, but she doesn't like ice cream.*

● Compose sentences with the children which consist of subordinate and main clauses and play about with the effects of changing the order of the clauses:

> *The band were awful because they were hungry and the bandleader was sick.*

> *Because they were hungry the band was awful and the bandleader was sick.*

> *The band was awful and the bandleader was sick because they were hungry.*

● Start with a sentence stem and encourage the children to extend it using different coordinators and subordinators:

> *I was hungry and…*
> *I was hungry because…*
> *I was hungry until…*

Resources

Listen to Your Child by David Crystal (Penguin) is a very readable guide to the development of vocabulary and sentence structure in young children's speech.

Inspirations for Grammar by George Hunt (Scholastic) is a compendium of activities for work at Key Stage 1 and 2, including many ideas for sentence-level work. (Please note, that this book is out of print, but is still available from some libraries and online book shops.)

Punctuation

The word 'punctuation' is derived from the Latin *punctuatio*, meaning 'to pierce or mark with a point'. This probably refers to the ancient practice of actually piercing a manuscript with a stylus in order to indicate boundaries between sentences or individual words. At a time when writing material was far more expensive than it is now, the use of blank space to mark such boundaries would have been an exorbitant luxury.

Up until the 17th century, punctuation was used to indicate how a spoken text might be read aloud by an orator. In an age before the spread of both literacy and access to published material, this practice was extremely important in disseminating information, instruction and literature for enjoyment. Early guides to punctuation, therefore, stressed its role in indicating pauses, metrical patterns and intonation, known as prosody.

Punctuation

Subject facts

Although there is some criticism of teachers who teach that the role of punctuation is to indicate where to pause if one were reading the text aloud, this prosodic function does have a respectable pedigree, and remains one element of punctuation use. It is clear that question marks, exclamation marks and brackets can act as indicators for the modulation of the voice. However, it would be misleading to present punctuation marks as merely pause indicators. In the 17th century Ben Jonson's *The English Grammar* set out guidance for the use of punctuation as an indicator of relationships between grammatical elements, and it is this syntactical function which is prevalent today. The demands of the voice and the ear in reading aloud are not always the same as those of the eye and the brain in comprehending a written text. When we are reading, we need to see which grammatical elements of the text belong together and which should be separated; this 'parsing' of the words and word groups on the page is what triggers our interpretation of the text.

Patterns of usage

Punctuation conventions differ across historical periods and from writer to writer. Moreover, the same writer can use different styles depending on such factors as the formality of the message, the identity of the addressee and the amount of time available for composing the message.

However, it is possible to overstate the extent of this flexibility. There are conventions which govern punctuation, but these conventions change over time, and at any one time there are freedoms available in punctuation which are not available, for example, in spelling. Nowadays, heavy and light styles of punctuation are equally acceptable, though the latter is much more prevalent than the former. Choices about punctuation involve thinking about nuances of meaning as well as about the overall degree of formality.

Why you need to know these facts

● Children's earliest hypotheses about punctuation seem to be that these marks are purely graphic, decorating the text or splitting it up into visual chunks, hence the prevalence of line ends or seemingly randomly distributed full stops in early writing. Children who are anxious about the placement of marks whose function they do not yet understand might be inhibited from writing at all if the importance of producing correct punctuation is stressed too soon.

Teachers need, therefore, to introduce punctuation to children in a way that is relaxed, informative and tolerant of early misconceptions. These misconceptions will probably be minimised if punctuation is approached first of all through the exploration of reading material (especially in shared reading sessions) and environmental print before it is required in writing. When it is introduced in writing, this should be during shared writing rather than in the course of solitary effort. Shared writing enables the scribe to make suggestions about the use and position of the relevant marks, reminding the children about what they have learned about them from their reading and observation of environmental print.

Vocabulary

Prosody – the structure of speech, including rhythm, stress, and intonation.

Common misconceptions

By the time children arrive in Key Stage 2, many (but by no means all) of them will have a working knowledge of basic punctuation. At this stage there is a danger that teachers will assume that use of the basic stops (full stop, comma, question mark and exclamation mark) will become automatic with accumulating practice, and that more complex conventions such as speech marks, apostrophes and semicolons, can be dealt with by teaching from rule books and worksheets. It will probably be more effective and motivating to continue to take an exploratory, even playful approach to punctuation, encouraging readers to research and discuss how marks are used in published material, and helping them to use punctuation to shape and reshape meaning and shades of meaning both in their own writing and in material that you prepare for them.

Teaching ideas

● When reading shared texts, point out punctuation marks and ask the children to speculate about what they are for. Listening carefully to and noting down their responses might provide you with some unexpected insights into children's hypotheses about writing. It should give you a useful idea of both the foundation you have to build on, and the misconceptions you might have to undo.

● From the start, it is a good idea to try to stress the role of punctuation in linking together adjacent words into groups that are separate from but related to other groups. It can be done in a relaxed and simple way, building from the natural curiosity that children have about these marks: *These words tell us what the pig did, so we need a mark to separate them from what the cow did, and we need another mark to separate the words about the cow from the words about the duck... Mrs Wishy Washy was annoyed here, so this mark shows us that she shouted at the animals...*

● When doing individual or group reading, point out punctuation and remind readers of what they have learned during the group sessions. It will be useful to encourage children to question differences of approach in the books that they read. For example, some children's books do not use quotation marks to enclose speech; some indulge in popular culture's tendency to multiply exclamation marks.

● Set the children the task of doing some detective work about punctuation marks in the print environment beyond the school. Sources such as advertising, junk mail and warning signs will provide varied raw material. Comics and newspapers, with their often unconventional and unrestrained use of punctuation, will also be useful sources. Tabloid journalism in particular is lavish in its deployment of question marks (a good opportunity for discussing the use of rhetorical questions), exclamation marks and dashes. Discuss the virtual absence of colons and semicolons in such sources. Other devices to highlight text meaning, such as the manipulation of typography or text layout, might also be spotted by the children. An environmental print 'safari', conducted as weekend homework or under the guidance of the teacher, should provide ample information about idiosyncratic uses of punctuation.

● Both journalism and environmental print can provide examples of the mishaps that can occur when punctuation is neglected. The following examples are authentic, and might be adapted for classroom use. The first is a headline in which a colon has been substituted for a verb such as *claims, says* or *discloses*; in the second, hyphens have been omitted:

Weekend's five fires started by the same culprit: fire chief.

Visit Cavendich Mcbrae: highland crook and walking stick maker.

● Help more accomplished readers to compare contemporary punctuation patterns with those in older texts such as Bible translations (in relatively early versions, such as the King James Authorised Version, colons and semicolons are used frequently, but quotation marks are absent) and extracts from the work of 18th and 19th century novelists. Having become familiar with changes in the way that texts are punctuated, confident writers can be challenged to rewrite older texts, rebuilding the clause structure and the punctuation to give a more contemporary feel. Or they can be asked to write or rewrite pieces of their own in the style of earlier literature.

● Another general strategy that can be used with older children is comparison between spoken and written language. Record snippets of impromptu talk and transcribe them with the class (bear in mind that even a skilled transcriber takes at least ten minutes to write out one minute of natural talk). Many people reading such a transcription are surprised at how fragmentary and full of overlaps and hesitations natural speech is.

● Children at Key Stage 2 are often interested by the ways in which language play can be used to explore ambiguities and variations in meaning. Many of the jokes which become popular among children of this age are based on such shifts in sense. This curiosity about playful language manipulation can be channelled into the exploration of punctuation as a way of shaping meaning.

An illustrative episode occurred when the managers of a golf course were dismayed to discover that the notices that they had posted along footpaths across the course had been sabotaged by a group of literate activists. Where the managers had posted:

PRIVATE LAND: NO PUBLIC ACCESS

the saboteurs had converted the sign to read:

PRIVATE LAND? NO! PUBLIC ACCESS!

While trivial, this episode is emblematic of the way in which playing with punctuation can highlight its role in making meaning and in disambiguating word strings which might be interpreted in different ways. Play will not be a substitute for teaching about conventions, but it can help to contextualise work which is often overdependent on exercises in which learners have to restore deleted punctuation from arbitrary texts. Such exercises can be helpful, but they work best if they are done collaboratively, with a teacher demonstrating to children how punctuation choices can create differences in meaning.

Capital letters

Subject facts

Capital letters are used to mark all proper nouns (that is, a noun that identifies a unique person, place, animal, event or institution). This covers a broad range of phenomena including:

● **Days of the week, months of the year, special days, periods and events:**

The last Saturday in September was a perfect day for an autumn picnic.

The Boston Tea Party preceded the Revolutionary War, and is one of the events commemorated on Independence Day.

● **Placenames:** Capitals are used for the full range of placenames, from planets down to street and pub names. Words indicating position or direction are not usually capitalised unless they form part of a placename, or are being used to give a name-like significance to one of the words:

In Western Australia we put ice in our beer. They don't do that in the North.

The Four Horseshoes pub and restaurant is situated one mile east of the A4074 at the junction of Hookend Lane and High Street, Checkendon, Oxfordshire.

The planet Mars and the Milky Way are just two of the celestial objects whose names have been stolen by confectioners.

● **Official documents:** They are used in the names of political parties, official documents, trade names and official titles:

The Monster Raving Loony Party was founded by Screaming Lord Sutch.

The Trade Descriptions Act forbade the use of such slogans as 'Guinness is good for you'.

● **Sentences:** Capitals are used at the beginning of sentences and of quoted sentences in direct speech:

Breakfast is the most important meal of the day.

Mum appeared at the bedroom door and growled, "Where is my breakfast?"

● **Nations, religions, languages:** They are used to denote nations, nationalities, religions and languages:

Buddhist   Mongolia   Cantonese   USA   Polish   Jewish

However, when names of nations become attached to common nouns, they often lose their capitals, though usage varies from text to text:

french toast   brussels sprouts   russian salad

● **Titles:** The main words in the titles of books, periodicals, songs, poems and other works of art should be capitalised:

Breakfast at Tiffany's   The Pit and the Pendulum

Daily Telegraph   *The Canterbury Tales*

● **Abbreviations:** They are used in acronyms and abbreviations of titles and organisations:

PhD   MBE   CBI   UAE

● **Poetry:** In most conventional poetry, the first words of each line are capitalised, whether or not they begin a new sentence:

> *On either side the river lie*
> *Long fields of barley and of rye,*
> *That clothe the wold and meet the sky;*
> *And thro' the field the road runs by*
> *To many tower'd Camelot.*

● **Informal use:** In very informal writing, capital letters can be used to emphasise exclamations:

> *I was walking down the street minding my own business when WHAM the smell of garlic hit me.*

> *Mum's growl changed to a howl: 'WHERE IS MY BREAKFAST?'*

Another informal use of capital letters is to lend ironic or facetious significance to words:

> *Fanny Craddock was not a good cook: she was a Great Chef.*

Why you need to know these facts

● Capitalisation is a practice which is vulnerable to fad and fashion, and the usage notes above are but a rough guide to the most consistent patterns. A stroll down a city street or a browse through a popular magazine will demonstrate a wide range of deviations from these conventional patterns. In the light of such diversity of usage, it is important that children are clear about the expectations that their formal writing should meet.

Capitalisation conventions differ from language to language. In German, all nouns, common and proper, begin with a capital letter. In French and Spanish, days of the week and months of the year are not capitalised, nor are language names in Portuguese. In earlier centuries, English used capital letters for a far wider variety of nouns than it does now.

● Beginner writers often use capital letters in seemingly inconsistent ways. It is important that young children are familiarised with relationships between lower and upper case letters through interaction with clear alphabetic displays, set at eye level, and through daily demonstrations of the use of the two cases through shared writing sessions led by the teacher. This should be accompanied by handwriting and labelling activities which focus on the distinction (for example, practice in writing one's own name and address, helping to write the day and date on the board, reading and labelling maps, recording the names and authors of favourite books and so on). Look out for children who consistently use capital 'B' or 'D' in the middle of words; this could be a sign that they lack confidence in choosing the orientation of the lower-case letter, and so revert to the more distinctive upper-case form.

● Helping children to compose their own ABCs of alliterative phrases or sentences is always a useful idea. If you can motivate them to create sentences which require the use of both upper- and lower-case letters, you will have an opportunity to demonstrate the different uses, and children will have a record of this instruction to keep for reference. For example:

A is for Arthur, Ali and Ann
Who ate all the apples in Amsterdam.
B is for Bina, Betty and Bram
Who bought all the balti in Birmingham.
C is for Cheryl, Carl and Cyn…

Though older children who require such practice might turn up their noses at composing ABCs for themselves, they might be motivated to produce one for an audience of younger children, and thus learn useful information during the production process.

● Encourage the children to collect as wide a variety of uses of capitalisation as they can from the print environment. They can then sort examples into a display organised into categories, and analyse the rationale behind different usages. A single newspaper would make a good starting-point for this, as would the range of officially provided notices and labels along a single residential street or on the interior and exterior walls of the school.

● Look at texts from a range of historical periods and languages, and invite the children to speculate on the reasons for different capitalisation conventions. In the 17th and 18th centuries, for example, many more classes of noun were capitalised than are capitalised now. A discussion of the criteria for this should help focus learners' attention on current conventions.

● Help the children to investigate the connotations of particular letters and letter groups as they occur in the print environment, online and in literature. How many shades of meaning can they find for the letter 'x' standing alone, for example? The letter 'x' can be found in activity books (where you could be asked to put a tick or a cross in an exercise); algebraic formulae; as a sign meaning 'forbidden'; and other instances. Do the connotations vary according to the case of the letter?

● Invite the children to create a logo and newsletter for their own school, class or club, exploring capitalisation in different font types as an option for the design of this material. The fonts available in a standard word-processing program should make an adequate starting point for this, which can be augmented by reference to books and websites on graphic design and calligraphy.

Full stops

Children's early ideas about full stops

Also known as the period or point, the main job of the full
stop is to indicate the end of a sentence (usually a statement).
Though seemingly the simplest of the punctuation marks to
recognise and use, many children find mastery of the full stop
difficult. We have all taught children who, having been introduced
to this convention, use it to mark line endings, or pepper the
page with dots in a manner which appears, to the reader, to be
random. These practices reflect the crucial fact that mastery
of punctuation conventions is closely linked with awareness of
the grammatical and prosodic features that these conventions
reflect. Therefore, the use of the full stop is closely tied up with
an understanding of sentence boundaries. This is not to say that
unpunctuated work indicates an inability to write sentences.
For example, look at the following sample of Year 1 writing:

> *Mashed potato is a very nice.*
> *food I think it is any.*
> *way because it tastes lovely.*
> *first you boil the potatoes then.*
> *you squash them with a big masher.*

It is clear that 'underneath' the punctuation there is a coherent
sequence of well-structured clauses. The difficulty is not in actually
writing the sentences, but in becoming explicitly aware of sentence
boundaries and in seeing that they are much more fundamental in
segmenting the prose than the merely visual boundaries created by
line endings. Once this task has been achieved, preferably through
oral work in shared reading and writing, the role of the full stop
in marking these boundaries will become clearer.

Later developments

This will not be the end of your difficulties regarding this
punctuation mark, however. You will probably be familiar with
types of writing like this:

My favourite meal is fish and chips. Especially from the chippy in Molyneux Drive. They use proper dripping there. And they give you lots and lots.

The errors in this sentence could well be the result of the writer over-relying on a prosodic strategy 'putting a full stop when you need to take a breath' or on the 'complete thought' criterion. What is required here is a discussion of alternative ways of punctuating the passage – this might form part of a guided writing activity, using extracts from children's writing as a stimulus.

Even in published writing by adults, there are controversies about the use of the full stop, reflecting the controversies we looked at in defining a sentence. Look at the passage below:

The hamper contained a cornucopia of delicacies. There were cheeses from France and from Italy. Wine from California and sherry from Spain. The best venison that the Scottish highlands had to offer. A gallon of Irish oysters and a side of Milanese ham.

Here the writer has deliberately adopted a 'catalogue' style of writing, giving each item or pair of items due prominence by isolating them between full stops. However, a purist would argue that nothing should come between two full stops but a formal sentence – that is, a group of words consisting of at least one main clause containing a finite verb. The correct way to separate the phrases describing the contents of the hamper, such a purist would argue, is with semicolons (see pages 129–31). Such purism would, however, outlaw many of the 'sentences' to be found between full stops in the works of writers as eminent as Dickens and Joyce.

Finally, in the case of reporting direct speech, it is indisputably acceptable to mark verbless stretches of discourse with full stops:

"What did you have for lunch?"
"A tuna sandwich and a yoghurt."
"What kind of yoghurt?"
"Wortleberry."
"I've never tasted wortleberry."
"Very wise."

Minor uses of the full stop

The full stop also has minor uses. In trios (as an ellipsis) it can be used to convey mystery, uncertainty or the tailing off of an utterance:

I touched the haggis again. And felt a heartbeat…

I could have the salami or the bologna…

We had three days' supplies left. After that…

An ellipsis can also be used to indicate that part of a direct quotation has been omitted:

The minister insisted that, "Only carefully sterilised sewage from the most respectable homes… has been allowed to re-enter the food chain."

A minor use of single full stops is to show that words have been abbreviated, and to separate capital letters in abbreviations. They are also used to separate numerals in dates, times and decimal numbers.

Why you need to know these facts

● The use of full stops is frequently assumed to be a straightforward matter. But it is important to appreciate that the use of this mark, as with all other types of punctuation, is as dependent on the style and intentions of the writer as it is on hard and fast rules.

Amazing facts

As early as the 15th century, writers were playing with the position of full stops in order to show how meaning could be altered by the placement of punctuation. The following snippet is adapted from a 'punctuation poem' on the nature of priests:

Trustworthy. Seldom to their friends unjust. Glad to help. No Christian creature willing to hurt.

Trustworthy seldom. To their friends unjust. Glad to help no Christian creature. Willing to hurt.

Handy tip

The question mark and exclamation mark are alternative ways of ending sentences. Remind children that it is superfluous to follow one of these marks with a full stop.

Teaching ideas

● Give children lots of practice in sentence-generating activities (see Chapter 1, page 14), highlighting punctuation conventions as the sentences are produced. For beginner writers, sentence frames are an excellent way of facilitating this. For example, children can be invited to orally complete simple frames like the following:

Sometimes I like to eat _____. At other times I prefer to eat _____. If I had to eat just one food for the rest of my life, I would choose _____.

As children provide the completions, write the three sentences out on a flip chart or whiteboard, showing that the full stops go at the end of each of the chunks of meaning rather than at the end of the lines. Emphasise that the children have expressed three facts about themselves, represented by three sentences, each marked off with a full stop.

● With older children, discuss alternative ways of organising writing through different uses of punctuation. You will need to use colloquial language (*Which of these versions sounds/looks better?*) as a foundation for introducing formal terms such as 'phrase' and 'clause'.

● Encourage accomplished readers to seek out 'verbless' sentences in their reading, similar to those in the hamper passage (see page 124). Ask them to try to identify the effect that the writer is attempting to convey. They might compare such passages with similar ones in which brief conventional sentences are used:

> *The cheese was placed upon the table. It reeked. It sweated. When knifed, it squirmed.*

Challenge confident writers to invent passages like the earlier one describing priests, and to show how punctuation changes can affect meaning.

Colons

Subject facts

The colon was once used to indicate a pause value less than that of the full stop but greater than that of the semicolon. In this respect it is largely redundant. When reading early works of literature in which this distinction was active (such as the Authorised Version of the Bible, or 17th and 18th century prose writers) it is difficult to appreciate the subtle nuances which differentiated the use of the colon and the semicolon. Nowadays, the colon is used mainly to mark the beginning of a list, summary, quotation or supplementary statement signalled by the preceding clause:

> *Before you attempt to make your first loaf, make sure you have the following equipment to hand: a mixing bowl, a bread board for kneading the dough, and a two-pound stainless steel or aluminium bread tin.*

> *The benefits of a moderate but varied diet can be summed up in one phrase: a healthy mind in a healthy body.*

> *An oft-quoted description of nouveau cuisine best describes my feelings about this school of cooking: the artistic arrangement of gravy stains on a plate containing more flavour than the meal it carries.*

Now that the main course was over, we faced the premium challenge of the evening: a dessert reputed to pack more calories than the blubber of the average blue whale.

Another use of the colon is in indicating a contrasting connection between two clauses:

The dull man eats to live: the wise man lives to eat.

Why you need to know these facts

● The colon, having lost its role as a pause marker between the full stop and the semicolon, is one of the most straightforward of punctuation marks. From the point of view of the history of English, it is useful to know that it once had a wider use than it does now. It is also useful to know that its current use extends beyond the simple function of introducing a list.

Teaching ideas

● In the course of the shared writing of procedural texts (recipes, instructions for making things and so on), demonstrate the list-preceding function of the colon.

● Highlight the role of the colon in introducing the completion of a sentence by providing the children with activities which encourage them to summarise, paraphrase, find or invent quotations. For example, after the reading of particular texts, ask the children to produce completions for 'stem sentences' like the following:

The main ingredients of the medieval peasant's diet were as follows:

The advantages and disadvantages of vegetarianism can be summarised thus:

I would like to summarise my feelings about mashed potatoes in five well-chosen words:

Semicolons

Subject facts

The semicolon is used to separate two or more clauses in a sentence which are potentially independent, but belong together within one sentence because they are closely related:

Beans on toast is a good example of a legume and grain combination; houmous and pitta bread is another; black-eyed peas with rice is a third.

Here, a comma would be too weak a stop to separate the clauses, but a full stop between each of them would produce too staccato an effect, disjointing the harmony of content.

A semicolon can also be used to precede a conjunction between two coordinate clauses in a sentence:

Dhal with chapatis is my favourite grain and legume combination; however, I sometimes prefer lentils and millet.

Where the second clause is subordinate to the first, a comma, or no punctuation at all, is preferable:

Dhal with chapatis is my favourite grain and legume combination, because it combines a wide spectrum of flavours and textures with the full range of essential amino acids.

Semicolons provide a good way of 'strengthening' sentences in which non-finite clauses are used to qualify a main clause. Compare:

Deep-fried battered chocolate bars are no longer the trendiest item on the traditional chip shop menu, fillets of farmed salmon having replaced them in this role.

Deep-fried battered chocolate bars are no longer the trendiest item on the traditional chip shop menu; fillets of farmed salmon have replaced them in this role.

There is nothing wrong with either the grammar or the punctuation of the first sentence; but the use of an independent clause in the second example produces a stronger effect.

Semicolons can also be used to separate phrases, as opposed to clauses, especially where these phrases are long and already feature commas in their own internal structure:

> We ate barbecued marmot whose liver was as flavoursome as smoked mackerel; strips of cold, fatty, boiled mutton; dumplings plump with oniony offal; hillocks of gritty, pea-studded rice, and plenty of plain white bread.

In the above example, two of the items listed contain internal commas, so to separate them as wholes with commas would be potentially confusing. Because the items are phrases rather than potentially independent clauses, it would be inappropriate to use full stops (but see page 123 regarding the listing function of full stops), which would also produce too fragmentary an effect in what is supposed to be a unified and cumulative list. The semicolon is very useful here as an item midway between the comma and the full stop.

Why you need to know these facts

● The semicolon is often regarded as a particularly arcane piece of punctuation. Understanding of its functions seems to require a sophisticated knowledge of clauses and phrases. However, it is a useful device for indicating close relationships between chunks of information, and its usage is not as complex as might be feared. The important thing to remember is that the writer has to think about exactly what they want to express before choosing whether to use a semicolon or an alternative signal of relationship, such as a comma, full stop or conjunction.

Teaching ideas

● Set children the task of detecting semicolons in a variety of types of reading material, and help them to work out why the author chose this stop rather than a full stop, comma or conjunction in the given context. Children could replace the semicolons with alternative marks and discuss the effect of the substitution. This would make a useful guided reading activity for confident readers and writers, but you need to bear in mind that semicolons are relatively scarce items.

● During whole-class shared writing, model the use of semicolons. Try not to be too dogmatic about rules of usage; stress that the use of this mark is often a matter of choice depending on the writer's intentions. Episodes in shared story writing which lend themselves to the listing of fairly elaborate descriptive phrases provide opportunities for demonstrating the use of semicolons to separate such items:

So the witch popped into her magic blender the fat of an old, dry skeleton; the laughter of a weeping statue; the sweat of a snowman; and two teaspoons of instant custard powder.

● In persuasive writing, creating a concise summary of points in favour of or in opposition to a position provides an opportunity to demonstrate the use of semicolons in separating closely related clauses:

My objections to the battery farming of poultry are as follows: the animals lead short, miserable lives; their living conditions lend themselves to the spread of diseases which are transmissible to humans; and meat produced by this method tastes like second-hand chewing gum.

Note that in such instances, it is usual to use a semicolon between the penultimate and final items, but a comma is also common.

Commas

Subject facts

It is often stated that commas are used to indicate a short pause in the course of a sentence. In fact, they are perhaps the most versatile of the punctuation marks, being used for a broad and potentially confusing variety of grammatical purposes, as detailed below.

● **List:** Words and phrases in a list or series are usually separated by commas. In a sentence such as:

The most nutritious fruits include blueberries, kiwis, strawberries, melons and mangoes.

commas are most commonly used after each item, up to the last but one. Sometimes a comma is used between the last but one and the *and* preceding the last item. This is uncommon, but not incorrect. The comma in this position becomes advisable when its omission could lead to ambiguity:

There were five items on the main course menu: roast duck, pork chops, lentil curry, haddock and chips, and macaroni cheese.

The omission of the comma before the final *and* could result in a potentially confusing expansion of the menu.

● **Adjectives:** Where the series consists of a set of adjectives qualifying the same noun, commas are generally used to separate these adjectives and to create a cumulative effect:

a hot, sweet, rich, soothing cup of tea.

An additional comma after *soothing* would be redundant and, if the writer wanted to create a brisker effect, the commas could be omitted all together. This would, however, be regarded as unconventional. Where the final descriptive term identifies the species of the noun, it should be treated as a part of the noun, and not be preceded by a comma:

a large, spicy, fragrant Manx kipper.

● **Bracketing:** Commas in pairs are used to give a parenthetic or bracketing effect to what they enclose. The word, phrase or clause enclosed may be an explanation in opposition to the preceding noun phrase:

Ugli fruit, a large citrus resembling a cross between a tangerine and a grapefruit, make delicious juice.

They may provide an optional commentary on the preceding item:

School dinners, at least in the opinion of those who eat them, are more interesting socially than gastronomically.

They may consist of adverbs or adverbial phrases which emphasise the writer's attitude:

Genetically modified foods have, fortunately, failed to inspire public confidence.

They may provide a contrastive element:

It was the quality of their rations, not of their weapons, which made the Allied troops so effective.

● **Enclosing:** A related 'enclosing' use is in setting off non-restrictive phrases and clauses from the rest of the sentence (see the section on clauses and phrases on pages 20–26). Compare:

Bananas, which are grown in the Caribbean, are highly nutritious.
Bananas which are grown in the Caribbean are highly nutritious.

In the first sentence, the enclosed phrase is non-restrictive: it provides a piece of optional information about the subject. It is not necessary to the basic meaning of the sentence, and is therefore placed in parentheses between the commas. In the second sentence, the phrase *which are grown in the Caribbean* is restrictive:

it implies that specifically Caribbean bananas are nutritious, and is therefore essential to the meaning of the sentence.

- **Subordination:** A comma is used to separate a long subordinate phrase from the main clause that follows it:

    Because deep-fat frying is a dangerous process, the preparation of fish and chips is not a suitable task for a minor.

- **Addressee:** A comma is used to separate the vocative or addressee of an utterance from the rest of the sentence:

    Lucy, what would you like to drink?

- **Connective or adverbial:** A comma is used to separate a sentence connective or adverbial from the rest of the sentence:

    Sweet and sour baked bean pizza is a triumph of fusion cuisine. Furthermore, it is cheap and easy to prepare.

    Yesterday, I ate my first raw egg since the salmonella scare of ten years ago.

In some cases, inserting a comma before the adverbial prevents a misreading of the sentence:

    While I was swallowing, a whole roast ox was placed on the table before me.

Without the comma, the impression might be created that a whole roast ox was swallowed. Similarly, though a comma between two clauses joined by *and* is not usually necessary it is required when a misreading might occur:

    Kathy fed the pigs, and the chickens were left to scratch up the spilt swill for themselves.

Without the comma, an inexperienced reader might assume that Kathy fed both the pigs and the chickens, and become confused by the rest of the sentence. These sentences are called 'garden path' sentences, because they can cause readers to become confused by making premature and erroneous judgements about their meanings. Careful punctuation can help to prevent this.

● **Addresses and dates:** Commas are used to separate items in addresses and dates:

> *The annual dinner will take place on Wednesday, 21 December at The Park Lane Hotel, Piccadilly, London WIJ 7BX.*

● **Speech:** Commas are used in conjunction with speech marks to separate the words used by the speaker from the reporting clause:

> *"When I get back to England,'"she sighed, "I'll dine on pork pies and mushy peas for a month."*

● **Pause:** A comma can be used to create a 'pause for effect' in a sentence. Compare:

> *He lifted the lid from the pot and found it empty.*
> *He lifted the lid from the pot, and found it empty.*

The use of the comma in the second example suggests that the emptiness of the pot is a shade more significant than it is in the first sentence.

● **Numbers:** Commas can be used to separate trios of numerals in order to make numbers over a thousand easier to read.

> *The average tea drinker will consume 102,000 cups of this liquid in the course of a lifetime. Serious tea addicts may drink up to 1,000,000 cups.*

Why you need to know these facts

● As with full stops, the uses of commas are a lot more complex than they first appear, yet this element of punctuation becomes a requirement very early on in primary education. Commas are particularly subtle customers because their use is governed far more by literary fashion and the style and intentions of individual authors than by agreed rules of usage. Compare the work of 19th century authors with those of contemporary writers and you will see that the comma is used much less now than it was then.

It is perfectly possible for two versions of the same text to include or omit commas at various choice points, and for both versions to be coherent and effective. So called heavy and light styles are illustrated below:

> *Dear Sir,*
> *I am writing, at my family's request, to thank you for the excellent meal which we enjoyed at your establishment, The Black Horse, last Sunday lunchtime.*

> *Dear Sir*
> *I am writing at my family's request to thank you for the excellent meal which we enjoyed at your establishment The Black Horse last Sunday lunchtime.*

● It is difficult for teachers feeling insecure about how to teach punctuation to appreciate that 'the rules' preached by prescriptive manuals are not as binding as language authoritarians pretend that they are. However, there are some clear and common errors in the use of commas which teachers can point out to children. For example, placing a comma between two independent sentences not linked by a conjunction:

> *Turkish food is magnificent, it has influenced the cooking of both Europe and north Africa.*

Here a semicolon or a full stop is essential; alternatively, the conjunction and could be inserted between the two clauses.

An 'opposite' error is to place a full stop, not a comma, before a sentence element which is not independent:

> *Turkish food is magnificent. Especially the use of fruit in meat cooking.*

Here it would be preferable to use a comma between the two chunks.

Another typical error is placing a comma between subject and predicate:

The question as to whether one should put the milk in the cup before the tea or the tea before the milk, is one which continues to excite controversy.

The writer's motive here is to provide a pause after a lengthy subject noun phrase, but it is not really needed. If the subject does grow to be so long as to create the need for a pause between it and its predicate, it is probably better to attempt to recast the sentence.

Occasionally the use of a single comma should be addressed where it would be better to use two or none:

The Lancastrian custom of using beef dripping to fry halibut should, in my opinion be made compulsory throughout the kingdom.

The comma should be either omitted, or a second comma added after *opinion* to place the comment in parentheses.

Be aware of the use of commas to enclose relative clauses which should be restrictive:

Kebab houses, which use substandard meat, are a public health hazard.

Here the sense conveyed is that all kebab houses use substandard meat and are health hazards. Omit the commas and the sense changes to only those kebab houses which use substandard meat are health hazards.

An 'opposite' error occurs when commas are omitted from relative clauses which are intended to be non-restrictive:

The management regrets the overcooking which was caused by an apprentice.

The implication of the missing comma, which should have preceded *which*, is that there were other episodes of overcooking that were not the responsibility of an apprentice that the management does not regret at all.

Questions

When do you use commas with *however*?
The word *however* needs a comma when it begins a sentence as a connective or is used in parenthesis:

Shrimps are becoming as scarce as oysters.
However, they are still surprisingly inexpensive.
They are, however, still surprisingly inexpensive.

However does not need a comma when it modifies a verb rather than the whole sentence:

However you interpret these figures, they still don't add up.

Handy tip

Note that it is usual to omit commas between two commonly adjacent adjectives preceding a noun:

A big red bus was approaching the bridge.

Teaching ideas

● Once children have encountered the basic patterns outlined above in their reading, it is better to provide them with examples of alternative usages, and to help them to appreciate the meanings and nuances thereby produced, than to teach hard and fast rules.

● Examine the use of commas in texts from different periods and genres. Compare mobile phone text messages, with their very restricted use of punctuation, with casual journalistic prose on the one hand and the composition of a classic novel on the other.

● Invite the children to make explicit the differences in meaning produced by different placements of commas, particularly with regard to restrictive and non-restrictive clauses:

> *School dinners are better than burgers which are full of cholesterol.*
> *School dinners are betters than burgers, which are full of cholesterol.*

● Pondering the effects of the use of commas as 'suspense points' within sentences is a more subtle process, but is worth doing with more experienced writers:

> *Eat jellied eels and you'll live forever.*
> *Eat jellied eels, and you'll live forever.*

● To highlight the use of commas to separate items in a series, present children with potentially ambiguous lists and ask them to produce alternative punctuation patterns. For example:

> *The larder louse is an omnivorous crustacean which will happily eat fruit pies paper napkins copper pots fish fingers onion rings chicken soup sugar soap and caviar.*

How many different items are mentioned in the larder louse's diet? The answer can vary from eight to fifteen depending on where the commas are placed.

● Let the children explore how commas can remove ambiguity in a sentence; ask them to insert or omit commas to produce alternative meanings.

Question marks

Subject facts

The main function of question marks is to indicate that the preceding sentence is a question – the upward curve of this mark, rising like an unfurling shoot, may have been an attempt to imitate the rising inflection of a spoken question:

> *Can I interest you in a knickerbocker glory?*

By extension, question marks may be added to sentences with the grammatical form of statements in order to indicate uncertainty, irony or incredulity:

> *He actually enjoyed eating it?*

> *So this is the fantastic meal you promised me?*

> *Surely you're not going to have a third helping?*

The question marks are essential here in order to represent the questioning tone which would be used in spoken language.
It is less acceptable to use a question mark to indicate a reported question:

> *I asked the chef if he could go easy on the hot peppers?*

This feels incorrect, because the sentence is a statement about my request. However, a follow up to the reported question standing on its own does need a question mark:

> *I asked the chef if he could go easy on the hot peppers. How would he like to have the tongue in his head stir-fried?*

Why you need to know these facts

● The grammatical form of a spoken sentence is often at odds with its real-life function. It is very common, especially in educational settings, to have statements which carry the force of questions or commands:

> *I wonder if there's any more custard in the jug.*

> *I can hear somebody slurping his milk.*

Apparent questions can also have the force of commands:

> *Who has forgotten to clear his plate away?*

Or they can act as statements expressing judgement:

Is that all I'm going to get?

When we come to express these usages on paper, the beginner writer needs to be aware that punctuation choices are available to clarify nuances of meaning.

Amazing facts

In Spanish, question and exclamation marks are placed at the beginning and the end of the sentence, the first one being turned upside down. This has the advantage of forewarning the reader of the grammatical status of the sentence.

Questions

How do you punctuate questions within sentences?
Sometimes questions can occur in lists in a mid-sentence position:

Questions such as how do I know this? how reliable is my evidence? how can I check my sources? are important ones in any research project.

Usage differs as to whether or not one should capitalise the first word of the question, and whether or not one should use commas between them (if the questions were placed within speech marks, commas would certainly be used). The model above avoids overcapitalisation and double punctuation, but it is not the only solution. A way round the issue would be to use bullet points:

Questions such as
- *how do I know this?*
- *how reliable is my evidence?*
- *how can I check my sources?*
are important ones in any research project.

Teaching ideas

● Encourage the children to collect examples of the types of form-function anomalies noted above, discussing how context and punctuation choices affect the meaning conveyed. Stock phrases in conversations between unequal participants (teachers and pupils; parents and children) can often provide reliable examples.

● The straightforward use of question marks can be demonstrated in shared writing. Most children catch on to their use quite quickly, and find their elegant shape appealing. Shared writing tasks which are engineered to demonstrate the difference between reported and direct speech (for example, transcribing an interview, followed by writing a summary of the interview) provide useful opportunities for demonstrating the conventions mentioned above.

Exclamation marks

Subject facts

Exclamation marks are used to represent utterances which in speech would require exclamatory force or raised volume, expressing either surprise, anger or some other strong emotion:

This wine is utterly superb!

What a pity you've lost your appetite!

I'm sick of you going on about food all the time!

The exclamation mark is one of the easiest marks to recognise and use, but it is probably as well to reserve its deployment for genuinely 'strong' utterances. Over-indulgence devalues a useful mark, and gives writing a sense of insincerity or gushy enthusiasm:

*We found a wonderful little tea shop behind the market in
St Helens! They sell genuine Eccles cakes baked on the premises!
And the tea is made with old-fashioned loose leaves!*

The doubling or trebling of exclamation marks is common in
informal writing such as comics and personal letters, but it is
definitely to be discouraged in more formal texts.

Why you need to know these facts

● Exclamation marks are another device that children latch on
to quickly and are eager to adopt. Consideration of how the
use of this mark affects the tone of the prose it is applied to is
essential in familiarising writers with different levels of textual
formality. These marks can be frequent in texts which children are
most familiar with; they are, however, regarded as inappropriate in
many of the genres they are expected to produce.

Amazing facts

In the mid 20th century, an attempt was made to popularise
a new punctuation mark which combined the effects of
question and exclamation marks to represent the tone of such
utterances as:

You've eaten how much ice cream?!

It consisted of an intertwined exclamation and question mark,
and was known as the interrobang. It did not catch on.

Handy tip

It is a good rule of thumb that in formal writing, such as essays,
job application letters and official reports, the exclamation mark
should not be used at all.

Teaching ideas

● Collect a wide range of text types, including comics, advertisements, different types of newspapers, popular fiction, classic fiction and a variety of non-fiction. Help the children to compare the frequency and functions of exclamation marks in the sample. You could also look at alternative strategies for representing exclamatory force in texts (for example, use of bold type or block capitals).

● Present children with a text in which exclamation marks have been used liberally, and help them to compare it with the same text in which they have been reduced or omitted. What is gained and lost by the editing?

● In the course of shared writing, give children the choice of using or not using exclamation marks, asking them to justify their decisions in terms of the effect they want to convey. Try to ensure that they have opportunities to make such choices in dialogue and commentary, fiction and non-fiction, poetry and prose.

● Children might be interested in comparing the interrobang with some of the emoticons popularised in email and text message communication, for example :-) to convey a happy message or :-(to convey a sad one. They could be challenged to design new punctuation marks to meet the needs of their own writing.

Parentheses or brackets

Subject facts

Brackets, sometimes called parentheses, are used to introduce into the flow of a sentence subordinate information in as unobtrusive a way as possible, permitting the discourse preceding and following to run on without too much interruption.

The sentence into which brackets are introduced should
be grammatically complete without them. Brackets may
contain comments, afterthoughts, exclamations, explanations,
illustrations or references to other parts of the text:

*Steamed asparagus (surely the only way to cook this noble
vegetable) is best served with a simple dressing of melted butter.*

*The asparagus plant (Asparagus officinalis) is a domesticated
version of a saltwater weed.*

The asparagus (oh woe!) had run out before we arrived.

*Blanched asparagus is popular on the continent (see pages
16–19 for an account of the blanching process).*

*Asparagus is a notorious diuretic. (This, however, might count as
a benefit to some people.)*

Note that in cases like the first sentence, the brackets serve as an
alternative to a pair of commas: it would be redundant to include
commas as well. Note also the position of the full stop in relation
to the last two examples. In the penultimate one, the parenthesis
concludes the sentence and forms a part of it; hence the full
stop is placed outside the closing bracket. In the last example,
the parenthesis is inserted after the closure of the main sentence
rather than being inserted into it. It acts as an afterthought which
forms a complete, free-standing sentence in its own right; hence
the full stop is placed inside the closing bracket.

It is not unknown for longer parentheses to contain internal
brackets adding commentaries on the content of the larger
insertion, but this practice is likely to be confusing and disruptive
to the sense of the main sentence.

Square brackets are generally used to add clarification within
direct quotations. They indicate that the words enclosed are not
a part of the actual quotation.

*To quote the words of Orwell, 'We may find in the long run that
tinned food [a relatively recent invention in the 1930s] is a more
deadly weapon than the machine gun.'*

● Brackets are a useful way of adding gloss and detail to a piece of discourse. Their overuse can, however, lead to a cluttered style. By their very nature, they interrupt the flow of information. Inexperienced readers who come across them, unaware of their 'by the way' function, may be distracted from the main meaning of the text by them, so it is important to teach explicitly about their uses and potential pitfalls. It is also important to stress that they can provide a very economical way of expressing in writing 'compressed' information which it would take us much longer to convey in speech:

> *Alfred the Great (849–900AD) was a warrior, writer, translator, legislator and cake-burner.*

> *Fried mussels provide a (the?) Belgian staple.*

In the first instance, the brackets save us from having to write 'who lived from 849 until 900AD'. In the second instance, which is an example of informal shorthand, the bracketed expression gives us a quick way of conveying the idea that, in the opinion of some people, fried mussels are the most important Belgian dish.

Handy tip

Brackets are punctuation marks in their own right and do not require 'out-riding' commas. Read the sentence as if the text in brackets is not present; the punctuation should remain the same as how it appeared in the sentence before it was altered by the insertion of the bracketed text. If a comma is part of the original sentence it should remain, but it should be placed after the closing bracket, never before the opening one.

Teaching ideas

● It is important that children are familiar with how to read bracketed material before they attempt to use this device in writing. During shared reading, present the class with examples of prose containing different types of bracketed comment, and make clear the essentially marginal (but potentially useful) nature of this material.

● Introduce the use of brackets in writing through shared writing. Stress that this is an optional way of adding information to a text, and that the information might be omitted or incorporated in alternative ways. Emphasise that if brackets are to be used at all, the material within them should be as brief as possible. Discussion of brackets might be a good way to introduce readers and writers to the use of footnotes and appendices.

Dashes

Subject facts

The dash can be used as an alternative to brackets in order to enclose parenthetical material. If this choice is made, usage follows the guidelines given for brackets above. However, the dash has a rather informal demeanour, and in formal writing it is probably better to teach the use of brackets.

More formally, the dash may be used as an alternative to the colon to explain or expand upon the preceding phrase or clause:

Vegetarians may be divided into two classes – those who avoid all animal material, and those who partake of dairy products.

Vegetarianism was virtually unknown in England during less prosperous times – for example, between the wars.

It may also be used to collect the items in a composite subject and bridge them to its predicate:

Steaks knitted from soya fibre, nut-stuffed sausages, raw bean salads – all gave early vegetarian cookery a very bad name.

In older texts, the dash was used in conjunction with the colon to introduce a list:

The items in the ration pack are as follows:–

In all of the functions above, the dash can be replaced by the colon acting alone. Where the dash is indispensable is in indicating an incomplete or interrupted utterance, particularly when writing narrative and dialogue.

I smelled the black pudding again; it couldn't possibly–

Personally, I thought I'd chosen an excellent turkey for Christmas, but – well, at least all of those poor people were insured.

"Mum, can I have some–"
"No! It will make you poorly."

The dash is also used to indicate excited repetition of words and short phrases in dialogue:

"Surely it's not – not the – not the – vindaloo?" she gasped.

Why you need to know these facts

● Like the exclamation mark, the dash is an item which is often overused. As a general purpose marker of pause, parenthesis and interruption, its use can save the hurried writer of a casual text the trouble of selecting the right mark. As such, it is a useful fall-back device, but learners should be taught not to import such a labour-saving strategy into more formal writing. The phrase we use to describe careless texts as being 'dashed off' should provide a mnemonic warning against overuse of the dash.

It is worth reminding learners that the name of this mark is derived from its earlier meaning of a swift blow (as in I'll dash your brains out) and was applied to punctuation to denote a hasty stroke of the pen.

Teaching ideas

● Show children examples of the dash used to indicate suspension or interruption and ask them to find similar examples in their own reading. Instances from adventure fiction should be plentiful. Use this to demonstrate appropriate genres for using the dash.

● Look at examples of 'casual' texts which have been 'dashed off'. Depending on the age and ability of your children, an extract from one of Byron's letters would be an interesting historical example, as the dash is virtually the only punctuation mark to be seen in long tracts of these manuscripts. Help the children to discuss this with a more conventional text and compare the effects.

Hyphens

Subject facts

In print, hyphens closely resemble dashes, being a fraction shorter in length. However, their functions are almost directly opposite. Whereas dashes denote a break in the flow of discourse, either through the insertion of parenthetical information, or through interruption or hesitation, hyphens indicate a linking together of information.

Linking word parts

One of the first uses of the hyphen that children encounter
is in linking word parts which have been broken at line ends.
Research into text readability has indicated, not surprisingly, that
such breaks disrupt the attention of beginner readers, who find it
difficult to track the word from line to line. Most reading material
for early readers takes this into account by using left-justified text
– that is, the right edge of the text follows a contour dictated
by whole-word boundaries. However, you should be aware that
when you are producing your own materials, or advising children
on the layout of their own writing, that word breaks at line ends
are best avoided. If they are inevitable, it is best to hyphenate the
word at a syllable or syllable/morpheme boundary rather than at
random, and the division should be as even as possible:

> *Sarah spent a fortune on the ingredients for her famous*
> *pea and ham casseroles, but they were invariably ine-*
> *dible.*

is less readable than:

> *Sarah spent a fortune on the ingredients for her famous*
> *pea and ham casseroles, but they were invariably ined-*
> *ible.*

Hyphens in compound words

A very interesting use of the hyphen is in separating the
morphemes of expressions that might be regarded as candidates
for future compound words. In English etymology, the words
we are familiar with as compounds, such as *breakfast*, *eggcup*
and *teapot*, usually go through a three-stage metamorphosis.
They begin their lives as separate but habitually associated
words (*break fast*; *egg cup*; *tea pot*). In the course of common
collocation, such word pairs become hyphenated, then eventually
the hyphen is deleted and a true compound is formed. This is
an untidy and uneven process, and at any point in time different
dictionaries or spellcheckers will disagree as to whether a
word such as *eggcup*, for example, should be presented as
a single word, a hyphenated word, or as separate words.
(American usage, incidentally, tends more towards hyphenation

and compounding; British usage tends to attempt to preserve the
separation of words for as long as possible.)

Linking whole words

A third use of hyphens is to link words together in 'frozen
phrases' used as adjectives or nouns:

> *The batter spatters streaking the walls attested to Sam's
> devil-may-care attitude towards pancake flipping.*

> *King Alfred was a jack-of-all-trades, but useless in the kitchen.*

> *The paella was plonked down in front of us in a very take-it-or-
> leave-it manner.*

The role of hyphens in making certain expressions clearer can be
illustrated by the following pairs of sentences:

> *Get me a chicken from the coop.*
> *Get me a chicken from the co-op.*

> *I cook twenty-odd meals a month.*
> *I cook twenty odd meals a month.*

Nouns in apposition

Hyphens are used to connect nouns in apposition which form a
single concept:

> *The new fridge-freezer won't fit in the kitchen.*

Prefixes

They are also used before certain prefixes:

> *I'm anti-hunting but still like to eat venison.*

> *How many non-vegetarians do we have at the table?*

> *I've over-indulged in olive oil again.*

> *Anybody super-sensitive to salt?*

Why you need to know these facts

● The hyphen is a useful punctuation mark, and the variability in its usage provides an opportunity to demonstrate aspects of language change to children.

Amazing facts

Hyphenation at the ends of lines can confuse readers by creating two unrelated words out of one:

for-age	just-ice	mist-rust
sea-son	leg-end	fat-her
sea-ring	pick-led	part-ridge
can-did	ant-elope	rag-out

Teaching ideas

● Encourage the children to brainstorm compound words and to speculate on their origins. This is particularly interesting in the case of older compounds whose derivations have become opaque. For example, it is not immediately clear that the word *wardrobe* originally meant a chest for protecting (warding) one's robes, or that a cupboard was originally a board on which cups were hung. Temporarily restoring the hyphens to such words can demonstrate their origins and help children to memorise their spellings.

● Remind the children to look for hyphenation in their reading and to observe differences in usage.

● Demonstrate the disambiguation function of the hyphen by giving children phrases like the following, and asking them to play about with meaning changes created by the insertion or omission of hyphens:

ancient duty free champagne
deep fried Japanese seaweed
thirty odd apple bearing trees
anti deer hunting campaign
long suffering fish shops

Speech marks

Subject facts

Speech marks (also called quotation marks or inverted commas) are used to open and close direct speech and quotations. They may be either single or double, American usage favouring the latter and British usage the former. Double quotation marks are also more common in handwriting. Traditionally, the double marks are reversed at the end of the speech or quotation, giving the appearance of '66 followed by 99'.

The tract of direct speech enclosed by speech marks is treated like a sentence in its own right; it is usually capitalised, and the speech marks are placed outside of other punctuation marks which belong to it:

Grandma said, "Eat your shellfish and your brains will bloom."

"Why do we always have fish on Friday?" Liam asked.

However, when a full stop, exclamation mark or question mark punctuates the main sentence, it is placed outside the quotation marks. Compare:

Matthew asked, "What's your favourite type of fish?"

Did he really say, "All fish tastes the same to me"?

Quotation marks are not used when reporting indirect speech, except to give a particular word or phrase special prominence:

Theo declared his biriani to be 'transcendental'.

It is important to stress to learners that only the speaker's exact words should be enclosed by speech marks:

He told me, "I was one of his favourite dining companions."

This is wrong because the enclosed words are not what would have been said. The writer should either omit the speech marks, or recast the sentence using the exact words spoken:

He told me, "You are one of my favourite dining companions."

Normally, a comma is used within speech marks when a quotation is interrupted by a reporting clause:

"This rice pudding tastes ambrosial," Amber sighed. "I could eat it by the bucketful."

When the reporting clause interrupts a sentence, the first word of the resumed quotation is not capitalised because it does not begin a new sentence:

"I assume," hissed Gregory, "that this fish was dead before you grilled it?"

When a quoted sentence consists of two clauses joined by a semicolon, the semicolon is placed after any reporting clause:

I have never tasted anything like this in my life; what on earth is it?

becomes:

"I have never tasted anything like this in my life," she murmured; "what on earth is it?"

If a quotation is preceded by a lengthy or formal preamble, a colon may be used:

Tracy looked from child to child sternly and in silence before addressing them thus: "I have never witnessed such repulsive table manners in all of my 43 years as a dinner lady."

In extended dialogue, it is usual to give each speaker a new line in order to improve readability. Frequently, reporting clauses are omitted, and the reader has to construe who the speakers are and how they are talking from the context:

"What will you have tonight, sir?"
"Is your excellent calamari still on the menu?"
"Yes, but the octopus is a better choice in my opinion."
"What will you have, Serina?"
"I was contemplating the Humber Haddock, but if that's a Mersey Cod I can smell, my mind is made up."

Where speech or quoted material extends over several paragraphs, it is common to open each new paragraph with quotation marks, but to defer the closing marks until the end of the last paragraph.

Quotation marks are omitted when the writer is reporting the inner thoughts of a character:

Tastiest piece of shark I've ever eaten, Mark thought. Wonder what it was feeding on down there in Davy Jones's locker? Davy Jones's limbs I should imagine. Best not to know.

Quotation marks are used to indicate that the enclosed words have been taken from another source:

This particular mushroom is known locally as 'chicken of the woods'.

They can be used to show that the enclosed words are special, such as quotations from other languages:

This type of cooking instils a real sense of 'joie de vivre'.

(Italic print is often used as an alternative in this context.)

They can be used as 'scare quotes' to indicate that the writer wants to distance himself from the term enclosed:

*I don't normally go for 'lean cuisine' but the fragrance was
very persuasive.*

When a quotation occurs inside another quotation, it is common
in British printing to use double marks for the 'outside' quote and
single marks for the enclosed quote, though usage varies:

*Barbara said, "Making your own filo is hard work; but 'sheer plod
makes plough down sillion shine' as Gerard Manley Hopkins
used to say."*

Why you need to know these facts

● The conventions for using quotation marks are quite complex
and children often have difficulty with them, especially when
they are trying to decide where to place additional punctuation
marks in relation to the inverted commas. It is important to
be clear about the conventions and their variations in order to
provide appropriate support for children who are learning to
write dialogue.

Amazing facts

Quotation marks are a fairly recent invention, and were
uncommon before the 19th century. They are not used in older
texts such as Bible translations, and their omission does not lead
to any lack of clarity in such texts. Because of the complexity of
the conventions governing their use, and because they appear
to be redundant, some eminent writers have eschewed them.
Both George Bernard Shaw and James Joyce (who referred
to quotation marks as 'perverted commas') preferred to mark
the start of a speaker's words with a dash. Children might be
encouraged to try this out and to see whether or not it affects
readability and clarity. However, this should not be seen as a
substitute for learning the conventions. It should also be pointed
out that quotation marks are not redundant since, like brackets,
they serve a function which is not available in speech. Consider

the following example:

> *Eddie preferred Scottish fast food to the more 'sophisticated' victuals available south of the border.*

If we were to attempt to express Eddie's attitude towards English food in speech, we would have to use the words *so-called* before the word *sophisticated*, or make a gesture showing speech marks with our fingers.

Teaching ideas

● Help children to work out the rules for using speech marks by encouraging them to observe and discuss how they are used in printed material, such as Big Books or shared stories. Note that practice can vary from publisher to publisher and, in books for younger readers, quotation marks are often omitted altogether. Underlining or highlighting spoken words and reporting clauses in different colours can help readers to identify how these are most often organised on the page.

● When children come to write dialogue, the time-honoured practice of getting them to write inside speech bubbles and then transferring the words to quotation marks is a good way of teaching them to separate off the exact spoken words to be enclosed.

● In order to illustrate the conventions about the placement of punctuation, encourage pairs or groups of children to make up dialogues which you can scribe during shared writing sessions, demonstrating the conventions en route.

Apostrophes

Subject facts

Apostrophes originated as a way of showing that one or more letters had been omitted from a word:

This steak should've been cooked for longer.
('ha-' omitted)

She'd have shared her last crust with anyone.
('woul-' omitted)

Don't even think of taking it out of the oven yet.
('-o-' omitted)

Dinner's at six o'clock.
('i-' omitted) ('-f' and 'the' omitted).

It is normal in formal prose not to make such contractions, except in cases like o'clock where the contracted form has become obligatory.

Apostrophes used to be used to mark the plurals of letters and numbers where it was thought the omission of an apostrophe would lead to ambiguity, but this has now fallen out of fashion (for example, 1990s, not 1990's). Perhaps this may help to eradicate the ubiquitous greengrocer's apostrophe:

We sell apple's, pear's and artichoke's.

The apostrophe is also used to mark possession, and it is in this role that it creates most uncertainty. In the case of singular words and plural words that don't end in '-s', the possessive apostrophe is placed before the '-s':

This grocer's prices are very reasonable.

The children's menu is refreshingly sophisticated.

The Women's Institute is having a barbecue today.

In plural words, the apostrophe follows the '-s':

The butchers' anger at the price of sawdust was intense.

When a word already ends in '-s' or '-ss', the possessive is usually marked by placing the apostrophe after the original '-s' or '-ss' and adding an '-s':

Jones's oxtail is juicier than Smith's.

The princess's appetite was astonishing.

The additional '-s' can be optional (*St James'* or *St James's*), so it is important to maintain a consistent approach within one text.

With possessive pronouns, such as *yours, theirs, ours* and *its,* the apostrophe is not used at all:

We'll taste yours if you taste ours.

However, it is used with the possessive pronoun *one's*:

The chilli does tend to incinerate one's taste buds.

Apostrophes are often used in old-fashioned poems to show omission from forms such as *o'er* (over), *e'er* (ever) and *o'* (of). Another use is to mark omission of aspirates and syllables when attempting to represent accents:

'Ow the 'ell did 'e get so 'ungry? 'E can't get the 'taters down 'is throat quick enough!

However, some writers would now regard this approach to representing non-standard speech as condescending.

Why you need to know these facts

● The apostrophe for possession has often been described as a redundant punctuation mark: remove it from texts and little would be lost in terms of clarity. However, the apostrophe is unlikely to vanish in the foreseeable future, so it is essential that children learn to use the mark correctly. The apostrophe for omission is a more useful piece of punctuation: words such as *can't, won't, she'll* and *he'll* would, if the apostrophe were omitted, become homographs of *cant, wont, shell* and *hell*.

Common misconceptions

Ignorance of the use of the apostrophe for omission can sometimes lead to spelling confusions. For example, incorrect forms such as *could of* and *should of* seem to originate in the writer's transcription of the spoken forms *could've* and *should've*.

Amazing facts

The possessive apostrophe came into being as a special case of omission. In Old English, possession was marked by adding a case ending to the noun, doubling the final consonant and adding '-es'. In modern English we would write *the man's dinner*, whereas the Anglo-Saxons would have written *the mannes dinner*. Over the course of time the additional '-n-' and the '-e' were dropped, and the apostrophe was put in to show where they had been.

Handy tip

Remind children that in formal writing an apostrophe is never required when *its* occurs; since abbreviations are not appropriate in such writing, the writer will always either write *it is*, or the possessive *its*.

Teaching ideas

● Make sure that children understand how abbreviated forms such as those mentioned above originate by comparing them with their full written forms. You should also point out that such forms are more common in speech than writing, and do not usually occur in formal texts.

● To alleviate confusion about the placing of apostrophes to mark possession, help children to make up and illustrate mnemonic phrases or sentences. For example, pictures drawn to show the difference between the boy's sausages (one boy) and the boys' sausages (more than one boy) can be kept in each child's writing folder for reference. A sentence such as It's incredible what an elephant can do with its trunk can be recorded to show the difference between the two uses of this spelling.

Paragraphs

Subject facts

Although paragraphs are not usually regarded as an element of punctuation, they do have a related function in grouping and separating units of meaning, and in organising the printed space so as to make overall meaning as clear as possible. Paragraphs, therefore, have both a graphic and a meaning function.

Traditionally, writers are supposed to start a new paragraph whenever they embark upon a new topic, or upon a new aspect to a topic. This meaning function is the foundation of the graphic function: in order to signal a change or development in theme (and to ease the eye through pages full of writing) a line of print or script is left blank between paragraphs, or the first line of each new paragraph is indented (this aspect varies, of course, from publication to publication).

It is important for learners to remember that the paragraph is, like the sentence, a unit of meaning rather than of length. It is possible for a paragraph to consist of only one sentence. When, as is usual, it is composed of several sentences, the sense of these should be quite tightly related. When a paragraph contains so many sentences that it grows to a length that is unfriendly to the eye, it can be broken down into smaller chunks. It is less acceptable to amalgamate short paragraphs into longer blocks which deal with relatively disparate themes.

Traditional style manuals teach that each paragraph should revolve around a topic sentence, typically the first, that proclaims the theme of the paragraph. Subsequent sentences provide support for, or elaboration on, this topic sentence:

It is generally agreed that a meal which presents a good spectrum of colours also presents a good spectrum of nutrients. Consider a simple salad of lettuce, tomato and carrots. The greenery of the lettuce signals the presence of iron and chlorophyll. The redness of the tomatoes proclaims an abundance of complex antioxidants, and the orange hue of the carrots is a sure sign that vitamins A and D are present. The entire repast will be saturated in vitamin C.

Here, the first sentence makes an assertion, and the following sentences support this assertion by analysing an example of the generalisation that it delivers. It is not, however, obligatory for the topic sentence to go first:

The redness of a ripe tomato is not merely attractive: it signals the presence of complex antioxidants. The verdant hue of a healthy young lettuce delights the eye, but it also proclaims an abundance of iron and chlorophyll. Carrots are beautifully vivid in their pigmentation, a vividness announcing rich reserves of vitamins A and D. **In short, a colourful meal is a healthy meal.**

Here, the first three sentences provide cumulative instances of a general rule which is announced at the end of a paragraph in a final sentence that draws a generalisation from the preceding ones.

It is even possible for a topic sentence to be embedded in the heart of a paragraph.

Tomatoes are red and rich in complex antioxidants. Lettuces are green and gravid with minerals. Carrots are orange and overflowing with vitamins. **A meal which is colourful is a meal which nourishes.** But this does not hold if the colours are artificial; a meal whose radiance originates from the laboratory will merely pollute the alimentary canal with its gaudy pigments.

Here, the topic sentence again condenses the import of the preceding sentences, but the writer has added a rider to qualify the generalisation.

There are deviations from these patterns. Sometimes the first sentences in a paragraph will tend towards a generalisation which will be refuted by the final focus sentence:

The radiant, golden flesh of a mango invites us to revel in its sumptuous flavour. The violet blood of the blackberry is as vivid as the sweet acidity of its taste. The rubicundity of the strawberry reflects the glory of its piquancy. **But the majority of nature's brightly coloured fruits would kill you slowly and painfully were you to succumb to their seductive showiness.**

In other paragraphs, the topic sentence is followed by a chain of qualifying sentences:

A meal which looks like it has been assembled from the stripes of the rainbow is usually pleasing to both the eye and the palate. *This is not to say that a simple plate of mashed potatoes and white fish is to be sneered at. A bowl of steaming porridge consumed at breakfast time is probably the best way to start the day. And, in my opinion, there is nothing better than white bread floating on grey gruel for supper.*

It is important to note that the formal, logical structures which are outlined above are idealisations which are infrequently realised in everyday published writing. Writers and editors often value the visual layout of the page above the logical organisation of sentences and paragraphs, especially in texts such as newspapers. In fiction, descriptive and narrative chunking rather than logical relationship is obviously the organising factor. In dialogue, each speaker is usually given a fresh line, no matter how fragmentary each utterance might be. However, considerations of content and logic should underlie formal, non-fiction writing, and apprentice writers should, therefore, be aware of them.

Why you need to know these facts

● The ability to divide lengthier pieces of written work into paragraphs is essential in order to ensure readability and to enhance comprehension. Although traditional organising principles are less adhered to in informal text, learners should have some sense of logical principles underlying writing, so that they might apply these principles in their own work.

Teaching ideas

- As with other types of punctuation, awareness of how to use paragraphing is best developed by studying how the conventions are used in published materials. Give children plenty of examples that show how text is blocked in a range of texts, including formal non-fiction, narrative and the popular media. Logical and visual principles can be identified, and different approaches compared. Children can identify and underline topic sentences, and try to work out how the other sentences in the paragraph relate to the main one. Always remember, however, that a lot of the paragraphs you will come across will not conform to the neat categories outlined above. Possible reasons for this should also be discussed.

- Provide children with various types of sequencing activity to do in order to enhance their awareness of paragraphing. At the simplest level, a published text can be cut into separate paragraphs and children challenged to reassemble it in a way which makes logical or narrative sense. At a more sophisticated level, individual paragraphs can be cut into sentences, the sentences shuffled and a logical reordering sought. Paragraphs which lend themselves to alternative arrangements might be particularly useful in this type of exercise.

- Writing frames are a reliable way of helping children to appreciate and become adept at the use of paragraphing and other forms of organisation in their non-fiction writing. These frames can indicate various types of genres, including persuasive, explanatory, and comparison and contrast, as shown:

Persuasive
These are three reasons why I refuse to eat foods containing sugar. Firstly, _____.
Secondly, _____.
Finally, and most importantly, _____.

Explanatory
The discovery of America changed the European diet in
several important ways. The most important
was _____. Another change was to do
with _____.
Moreover, _____.

Comparison and contrast
Although _____ and _____ are
similar in many ways, in other important respects they are
different. Both _____ and _____
have/are _____. They both _____
and _____. However, while _____,
this is not true of _____.

Note that these frames will teach only a limited number of
paragraph types. The need to cue content at the beginning
will usually lead to the topic sentence being put first. You can
show children that this is not the only possible arrangement by
giving them potential topic sentences on appropriate subjects,
and helping them to build paragraphs in which accompanying
sentences precede or surround the topic sentence, supporting,
opposing or qualifying it:

1. _____
2. _____
3. _____
In short, the typical Anglo-Saxon diet was every bit as
healthy as the diet you have today.

(Sentences 1, 2 and 3 should support or exemplify the
topic sentence.)

1. _____
2. _____
3. _____
However, the diet we enjoy today is no better in nutritional terms than that endured by the Anglo-Saxons.

(Sentences 1, 2, and 3 should imply a contrast with the topic sentence.)

1. _____
2. _____
The typical Anglo-Saxon diet was simple, rough and monotonous.
However, _____
Moreover, _____

(Sentences 1 and 2 should exemplify or support the topic sentence; the last two sentences should qualify the topic sentence.)

You should guard against writing frames becoming strait-jackets rather than supports. Frames should be used temporarily to help children to organise their writing, with the eventual aim of being able to do this without such support.

Resources

Any Big Books which use a range of punctuation marks, especially speech marks with accompanying question and exclamation marks, are excellent visual resources for demonstrating punctuation usage.

Mind the Stop by GV Carey (Penguin) is an old-fashioned and prescriptive but still very useful guide to conventional punctuation usage.

Punctuation in the Primary School by Nigel Hall (RALIC/University of Reading) is a short, concise guide to the development of children's knowledge about punctuation.

Glossary

Adjective – a word expressing an attribute of a noun, for example *a **ripe** banana*. Adjectives are usually gradable: *ripe, riper, ripest*. These grades are respectively known as the absolute, comparative and superlative forms of the adjective.

Adjective phrase – a phrase in which the main word or head is an adjective.

Adverb – a word which can modify a verb, an adjective or another adverb: *He walked **quickly**; he felt **extremely** uncomfortable; he breathed **quite** rapidly*. Adverbs can also join sentences together or provide a comment on the content of a sentence: ***Consequently**, he became tired quickly. **Frankly**, I became impatient*.

Adverb phrase – a phrase in which the main word or head is an adverb.

Adverbial – a clause element consisting of a word, phrase or clause which provides information about the verb in a sentence. Adverbials are usually optional in sentences, but some verbs would be incomplete without them: *Dinner lasted **until midnight**. She put the crumble **in the oven***.

Aspect – the element of a verb referring to how the action of the verb should be regarded in terms of its completion or duration: *He **had eaten** already but **was contemplating** a second helping*. The two verbs in bold both refer to past time but differ aspectually.

Auxiliary (helping verb) – verbs which occur with main verbs, serving to indicate aspect or modality.

Clause – a potentially independent string of words consisting of at least a subject and a predicate.

Command – see imperative.

Complement – a clause element which completes the meaning of either the subject or object in a sentence: *Elsie is **a baker**; she considers her loaves **exceptionally nutritious**.* The first bold element is a subject complement; the second an object complement. (Note that this term is also used more broadly to refer to any structure that completes another within a sentence. For example, in SVO and SVA sentences, the object and adverbial respectively complement the verb; in a prepositional phrase, the noun phrase is a complement to the preposition.)

Complex sentence – a sentence consisting of a main clause accompanied by one or more clauses which are dependent upon the main clause: *She kneaded the dough **because she needed the dough**.* The clause in bold in this complex sentence depends for its meaning on the initial clause.

Compound sentence – a sentence consisting of two or more coordinated main clauses.

Conjunction – a word which joins together words, phrases or clauses within sentences.

Coordinate clause – a clause forming a part of a compound sentence in conjunction with one or more clauses of equal status.

Copular (linking verb) – a verb which links a subject to its complement, for example, *be, seem, appear, become, sound, feel, grow, turn* and *remain*.

Determiner – a word occurring before a noun, indicating whether it is definite, indefinite, singular, plural and so on, for example *a, the, our, these, both, each* and *every*.

Ellipsis – the omission of words, phrases or clauses from sentences in the interests of coherence and economy. The ellipted (or elided) elements can be derived from the context: *Is that Holly's meringue? No, it's Oliver's…*

Finite/non-finite – a finite verb form changes according to tense: *He eats regularly; he ate a good meal every hour on the hour.* A non-finite form does not express tense: *Having eaten, he drank; having eaten, we will relax.*

Imperative – a sentence form expressing an order or directive. The subject is usually deleted.

m-p

Modifier – an element in a phrase occurring before or after the headword which adds to the meaning of that word: *The **gleaming** crockery **on the table** was immaculate*. The headword *crockery* in the subject noun phrase is premodified by the adjective *gleaming* and post-modified by the prepositional phrase *on the table*.

Noun – a word which usually names people, places, things and ideas.

Noun phrase – a phrase in which the main word or head is a noun.

Object – a clause element usually following the subject and verb and identifying either the entity which has been affected by the verb (the direct object) or the recipient of the action (the indirect object): *I gave **the soup** (DO) to **Charlie** (IO)*.

Participle – participles are words derived from verbs but serving additional functions. The '-ing' participle is often known as the present participle and can be used as an adjective and noun: *I bought her a **fishing** rod because she loves **fishing***. The '-ed' participle is known as the past participle and can be used as an adjective: *The **baked** trout was sumptuous*.

Passive – in a passive sentence the subject is the entity affected by the verb. The verb form changes and is accompanied by an auxiliary. In the following example, an active sentence is accompanied by its passive form: *The dog ate the meringue. The meringue was eaten by the dog*. Passive sentences allow the agent of the action to be omitted: *The meringue was eaten*.

Phrase – a string of words acting as a clause element. A phrase is named after the word class of its main word or head.

Predicate – the string of words following the subject of a sentence, consisting of at least a verb and frequently an object, complement and adverbial.

Preposition – a word occurring before a noun or noun phrase showing how the noun is related to other elements in the sentence.

Prepositional phrase – a phrase consisting of a preposition followed by a noun phrase.

Pronoun – a word that is used to replace a preceding noun or noun phrase.

Prosody – the structure of speech, including rhythm, stress, and intonation.

Relative clause – a subordinate clause which either provides optional information about a preceding noun phrase (a non-restrictive or non-defining relative clause), or which restricts the reference of the main clause to that particular noun phrase (a restrictive or defining relative clause). *My brother, **who lives in Kingston**, is a mushroom expert.* (Non-restrictive.) *My brother **who lives in Kingston** is a mushroom expert.* (Restrictive.)

Sentence – a string of words consisting of at least one clause, expressing a statement, question, imperative or exclamation.
Subject – a clause element usually preceding the predicate and identifying the theme, topic or agent of the sentence. In passive sentences the subject is the entity affected by the verb.
Subordinate clause – a clause in a complex sentence which is dependent on a main clause. (See complex sentence.)

Tense – variation in verb form to express the time frame of an action or event.
Transitive/intransitive – transitive verbs require an object: *Fido enjoyed the meringue.* (The sentence would sound incomplete without the object.) Intransitive verbs do not require an object: *Fido growled.*

Verb – a clause element identifying an action, state or relationship.
Verb phrase – a phrase in which the main word or head is a verb.

Index

co–mo

pu–ve